PRAYER

THE PROBLEM OF DIALOGUE WITH GOD

pRAYER

the problem of dialogue with God

PAPERS OF THE 1968 BEA INSTITUTE SYMPOSIUM

EDITED BY CHRISTOPHER F. MOONEY, S.J.

PAULIST PRESS

Paramus, N. J.   New York, N.Y.
Toronto   London

NIHIL OBSTAT:
Joseph F. Fitzpatrick
Censor Librorum

IMPRIMATUR:
✠ Thomas A. Boland, D.D.
Archbishop of Newark

July 30, 1969

The Nihil Obstat and Imprimatur are official declarations that a book or pamphlet is free of doctrinal or moral error. No implication is contained therein that those who have granted the Nihil Obstat and Imprimatur agree with the contents, opinions or statements expressed.

BOOK DESIGN:
Russetta Madison

Library of Congress
Catalog Card Number: 78-92220

Published by Paulist Press
Editorial Office: 304 W. 58th St., N. Y., N. Y. 10019
Business Office: Paramus, New Jersey 07652

Printed and bound in the
United States of America

contents

pREface

The six papers collected here were delivered during a three-day "Symposium on Prayer," attended by some two hundred people and held at Loyola College, Shrub Oak, New York, at the end of August 1968. The symposium was sponsored by the Cardinal Bea Institute, whose general purpose is to provide a forum on the university level where the religious values in American life can be discussed and the meaning of religious existence in a changing world clarified. Through a planned series of lectures and faculty seminars, as well as through symposia on special problems, it seeks to search out in advance those new forms which the spiritual life may in the future be called upon to take.

The crisis in prayer today is a reflection of the crisis in faith. Christians are being forced to rethink the nature of prayer as well as its significance in their lives because they have been forced to rethink what they believe about God. The problem of dialogue with God is thus the problem of God's relationship to man. On the one hand, Christian faith has always insisted that the world of men is God's world, the object of his care and concern, where he is continually present both as creator and redeemer. But the same faith has also insisted upon the divine presence in the heart of man, upon the intimacy between God and man made possible through Jesus Christ. How then, given his new understanding both of the universe and of himself, is the Christian to think today of this twofold divine-human relationship, the one in the realm of creativity and action, the other in the depths of the human heart?

If there was a single overriding corporate concern throughout the discussions at Shrub Oak, it was precisely this desire to know both how to think about prayer as well as how to pray in function of the human, that is to say, in terms of man's development as a person and as architect of the world around him. Bernard Lonergan has said, with his usual insight, that divine revelation is God's entry into man's making of man, and this can be said also of the contemporary experience of prayer. The difficulty today, however, is that we have not yet been able to evaluate or even to articulate the multiple elements which constitute this experience. In general, Christians do not want their religion or their religious practices in any way to separate them from the mainstream of human life. They desire their Church to embrace the whole of mankind. And they want both world and Church to move toward Christ not in parallel lines but by an interpenetration, an osmosis, as Edward Schillebeeckx has called it, so that, while the Church keeps her sense of identity as the Body of Christ, the boundaries between herself and the world become permanently blurred. Blurred, too, as a consequence would be distinctions between sacred and secular, religious and profane. To be credible today, the Church cannot stand apart from the world any more than Christ did through the incarnation; nor can creation ever be considered alone, complete in itself, independently of its elevation through grace.

More than once during the Symposium it was pointed out that no single person better symbolizes this concern for the human in one's life of prayer than Pierre Teilhard de Chardin. The style of prayer he developed in his own life was in fact an outgrowth of his desire to have a genuine experience of God in the midst of a world where God was thought irrelevant. The source of this experience he felt must be the divine presence and action at the heart of man's efforts to build the earth. This is why his frequent treatment of the theme of God's presence is of a piece with his efforts to rethink within an evolutionary world view the meaning of God's existence. For in the case of modern man, it is only within such a world view, focused upon the future and upon man's achievement as man, that God can be spoken about and encountered in adoration and prayer. The world must see, insisted Teilhard, that in the Christian, the horizontal dimensions of human life can be reconciled. His prayer must thus take place before God in confrontation and with God in cooperation. Such prayer must be made in hope as well as in faith, for God is present precisely in the future that man is now making, and he will meet him there each day at that point where human action is most creative.

All prayer, therefore, is in part an anticipation of the parousia, a form of expectation, an adherence in the present to that which we believe and hope will be realized in the future. Such anticipation is no compulsive figment of the imagination by which we pretend that things are not what they really are. Rather, as Peter Baelz has said, it is a contemplation of their present actuality within the context of the reality of the eternal purposes of God; a seeing of the world and of our neighbor in the light of the new creation in Christ. Because it flows from a recognition of what God has already done in and through Christ, such prayer will always have the aspect of penitence and thanksgiving. And because it looks forward to what God has still to do in and through those who respond to his love, it will always have the aspect of petition and intercession. Prayer as anticipation is thus both a resting in God and a wrestling with God, a tension between the "already" and the "not yet" which characterizes the whole Christian experience. And because his prayer is "not yet" perfect, the Christian offers it in the name of Jesus, whose perfect offering he now shares.[1]

In the pages that follow it will readily be seen how concerned were the speakers at the Shrub Oak Symposium for all the above problem areas insofar as they impinge upon the contemporary experience of prayer. The different points of view which they take is sufficient indication of how diverse the response of the individual Christian can be. Rev. Ladislas

[1] Peter Baelz, *Prayer and Providence* (London, 1968), pp. 99-102.

Orsy, S.J., who acted as coordinator for the Symposium, saw to it that the speakers chosen did in fact represent quite different backgrounds and even different traditions in Christian spirituality. The editor owes him a special debt of gratitude for the essential part he played in the Symposium, as well as for his advice on countless details and related problems. Both of us wish also to thank Rev. John Dineen, S.J., President of Loyola College, for his warm hospitality and enthusiastic cooperation, and Mrs. Helen Zeccola, the Institute's secretary, without whom nothing would ever get done.

Christopher F. Mooney, S.J.

can man encounter god today?

THOMAS E. CLARKE, S.J.

In this congenial assembly of simple people—simple philosophers, simple Bible Christians, simple monks and simple Jesuits, the only appropriate way for me to begin is to say that my name is Charlie Brown. And while I'm at it—so that this Bea Institute Symposium on prayer may qualify as an officially and authentically Roman Catholic enterprise—I must describe for you the latest Charlie Brown poster I've seen. Charlie is saying: "No problem is so big or so complicated that it can't be run away from." Let that stand as an appropriate text for these remarks on the problem of prayer.

More than one of the speakers at this symposium may have trouble fitting an abundance of inspiration into the limitations of an hour's session. My difficulty has been just the opposite, and so I am going to begin with the best part of this paper, several minutes of brilliant and provocative thoughts by persons other than myself. My purpose here, before presenting some reflections of my own, is to foster the attitude in all of us which is appropriate to our theme. We are not talking about prayer as we would talk about the structure of the molecule or the eating habits of the fruit-fly, but rather about something which is part of ourselves as persons, which we *are* as Christian persons, something which we all do, and do rather badly and something which we want to do better. Well, unless I am mistaken, that something we are doing, perhaps unconsciously, even as we talk and listen. And so, I suggest, as we listen now to some eminent men of prayer, let us pray. I will not be deducing anything from these quotations, or even be commenting on them. I do not offer them as representing, necessarily, my own view. All of them, however, have something to do with what I shall be saying.

• In our era, the road to holiness necessarily passes through the world of action.[1]

• For him who has not suffered, the brother does not exist.[2]

• Two and two only absolute and luminously self-evident beings, myself and my creator.[3]

7

• *Augustine:* Lo, I have prayed to God. *Reason:* Now what do you want to know? A. All these things which I prayed for. R. Sum them up briefly. A. I desire to know God and the soul. R. Nothing more? A. Absolutely nothing.[4]

• And what is this God? I asked the earth and it answered: "I am not he," and all things that are in the earth made the same confession . . . I said to all the things that throng about the gateways of the senses: "Tell me of my God, since you are not he; tell me something of him." And they cried out in a great voice: "He made us." My question was my gazing upon them, and their answer was their beauty . . . I asked the whole frame of the universe about my God, and it answered me: "I am not he, but he made me."[5]

• We must face up to the fact that the call of Christ *does* set up a barrier between man and his natural life . . . By calling us he has cut us off from all immediacy with the things of this world. He wants to be the center, through him alone all things shall come to pass . . . *He is the Mediator,* not only between God and man, but between man and man, between man and reality. . . . Wherever a group, be it large or small, prevents us from standing alone before Christ, wherever a group raises a claim of immediacy it must be hated for the sake of Christ. . . . For the Christian the only God-given realities are those he receives from Christ. . . . The path . . . to the God-given reality of my fellow man or woman with whom I have to live leads through Christ, or it is a blind alley. . . . Christ stands between us, and we can only get in touch with our neighbors through him. That is why intercession is the most promising way to reach our neighbors, and corporate prayer, offered in the name of Christ, the purest form of fellowship. . . . Though we all have to enter upon discipleship alone, we do not remain alone. If we take him at his word and dare to become individuals, our reward is the fellowship of the Church.[6]

• When we come before God with hearts full of contempt and unreconciled with our neighbors, we are both individually

and as a congregation worshipping an idol. . . . There is therefore only one way of following Jesus and of worshipping God,
and that is to be reconciled with our brethren.[7]

• I should like to speak of God not on the borders of life but
at its center, not in weakness but in strength, not, therefore,
in man's suffering and death but in his life and prosperity. . . .
God is the "beyond" in the midst of our life.[8]

• God is teaching us that we must live as men who can get
along very well without him. The God who is with us is the
God who forsakes us. The God who makes us live in the world
without using him as a working hypothesis is the God before
whom we are all standing. Before God and with him we live
without God. God allows himself to be edged out of the world
and on to the cross.[9]

• Now that it has come of age, the world is more godless, and
perhaps it is for that very reason nearer to God than ever
before.[10]

• There is always a danger of intense love destroying what I
might call the "polyphony" of life. What I mean is that God
requires that we should love him eternally with our whole
hearts, yet not so as to compromise or diminish our earthly
affection, but as a *cantus firmus* to which the other melodies
of life provide the counterpoint. Earthly affection is one of those
contrapuntal themes, a theme which enjoys an autonomy of
its own. . . . When the ground bass is firm and clear, there is
nothing to stop the counterpoint from being developed to the
utmost of its limits.[11]

• By means of all created things, without exception, the divine
assails us, penetrates us and moulds us. We imagined it as
distant and inaccessible, whereas in fact we live steeped in
its burning layers. *In eo vivimus.* As Jacob said, awakening from
his dream, the world, this palpable world, which we were wont
to treat with the boredom and disrespect with which we habitually regard places with no sacred association for us, is in truth
a holy place, and we did not know it. *Venite, adoremus.*[12]

With these texts, and the various resonances they may evoke in each one of us, I would like now to circle around the question posed in the title of this paper: Can Man Encounter God Today? Let me begin by suggesting that, at least in Roman Catholic circles, the crisis of prayer and faith has come about, in large measure, from the meeting and clash of two very different viewpoints: the theology and spirituality of sacramentality (conceived as encounter with God and Christ), and the theology and spirituality of secularity. More than a decade ago, due to the influence of ecumenism, personalistic philosophy and other currents of thought, Catholic theology bade an unfond farewell to the post-Tridentine accent on *ex opere operato*, judged to be dangerously open to mechanistic or magical interpretations, and began to speak of our encounter with Christ in the sacraments and in the whole life of the Church. Edward Schillebeeckx's little masterpiece[13] was undoubtedly the principal agent, at least in this country, of disseminating this thrilling new and personalistic expression of Christian sacramentalism. The influence of Teilhard extended the range of this encounter with the divine to the whole of the evolving cosmos, conceived as the diaphanouse, epiphanic milieu which throbbed with the presence of God. Vatican II reflects very strongly this reawakened sense of the divine presence throughout the whole of human and cosmic life.

But hardly had we finished proclaiming the joyful message that God and his Christ were to be encountered everywhere when we became aware of other voices, announcing that the God whose presence we were celebrating was really an absent God; that the God to whose revealing sacramental word we were responding in joyous faith was really a silent God, a God who does not speak to man; and in fact, that the living God who called us to life had really died, as Nietzsche had proclaimed. Even though many versions of the absence, silence or death of God were not properly atheistic, the very least that this current of secular Christianity would settle for was that he was a God who was totally Other, not to be encountered. His very otherness was, for some like Friedrich Gogarten,

a liberation of man to do his rational thing in the world un-
hindered by intrusion from inhibiting or distracting deities,
as in ancient paganism. But in any case it was futile, if not
blasphemous, for man to look to God as a dialogue partner
within the finiteness of daily human existence.

The implications of such a challenge to a spirituality of
encounter were plain. And the doubts regarding prayer that
began to afflict many Roman Catholics, particularly priests and
religious, were not merely whether the God-encounter in interpersonal relations and social action was now sufficient without the God-encounter of formal prayer, but whether God was
to be encountered at all, whether Christ was to be encountered
at all. On this last point many felt, quite wrongly or at least
quite oversimply, that critical study of the Gospels had taken
away the Jesus of history; and as for the glorious Christ—well,
encounter with him seemed as much an impossibility as
encounter with God.

It was not merely the theology of secularity which disturbed
the spirituality of encounter; the picture is more complex.
The scientific world view, with its progressive and inexorable
erosion of the divine beachhead in the world of nature and
of man, was an important factor. But it is unlikely that this
triumph of the scientific world view alone would have so
shaken the foundations. Among many influences, the ever more
patent inability of the Church and her theologians to meet
the new problems raised regarding accepted dogmas of faith
and regarding an immutable natural law tended to bring dis-
turbing doubts where previously there had been only assurance
of divine guidance through the Church. And the "last hurrah"
(still echoing) of a centralized, uncollegial and rather fearful
bureaucracy has not helped; neither have some of the excessively shrill denunciations of it. But, most of all, the terrible
evils of the last fifty years—Dachau and Vietnam and American
cities in flames—have left most of us silent or stammering in
the face of the obvious question: Where is your God? Where is
the Christ you claim to encounter?

This, it seems to me, is where we are now: not merely

addressing in a new context the perennial problem of contemplation and action, but asking ourselves whether the theology and spirituality of God-encounter and Christ-encounter are really viable, or whether they must yield to a theology and spirituality in which man is alone in his work in the world, at least so far as any experience of God is concerned. Can man today really encounter God, either in formal prayer or in standing with his neighbor?

My very small contribution to an answer to this question is to suggest, first, that a more adequate answer will be strongly qualified Yes; that the qualification is to be made with help from the theological and mystical traditions; and that more distinctively contemporary expressions must be found for these traditional expressions of Christian faith.

My impression is that the theology and spirituality of the encounter with God and Christ have suffered from expecting both too much and too little: too much in the sense of not taking with full seriousness that this is an encounter in the darkness as well as in the light of faith; too little because the God and the Christ who tended to emerge as dialogue partners in the encounter were a diminished God and a diminished Christ, not the *Deus semper maior* nor the Christ whose riches are unfathomable. And if encounter spirituality is to sustain the meeting with secular Christianity, it is in need of speedy help from two interrelated streams of Christian tradition: the theological tradition of the negative theology and the spiritual tradition of the dark night.

Let me seek only to identify rather than to analyze this twofold tradition. The negative theology formulates the biblical teaching and the Christian experience of the mysteriousness and transcendence of God in such terms, familiar to many of you, as: We know of God rather what he is not than what he is; we know that God is, but not what he is or how he is, etc.

Frequently the austerity of this negative theology is domesticated by appeal to the Incarnation, to the fact that, incredibly, the God who is totally Other has spoken to man in Christ, in whom the Father's image is manifest to us. This is undoubtedly true, if properly understood. But this manifesting Word which is Christ is itself unfathomable, and to the negative theology we must add a negative Christology, so that we may say in truth: We know of Christ rather what he is not than what he is. The disciple of Christ has not less but more appreciation than anyone else that the God of our Lord Jesus Christ and Jesus Christ himself in glory are not to be encountered in the way in which we encounter other human beings.

We may perhaps even go a step further, and to the negative theology and negative Christology add a negative anthropology. Are we so sure that we really do encounter the neighbor? Joseph Pieper has brought out in his little work, *The Silence of St. Thomas,* that the creature as creature is mystery to us, and somewhere, I think, St. Augustine has said that it is only in eternity that we will really see the neighbor, when we see him in God.

The mystical corollary of this negative theology is the spirituality of the dark night. As I understand its expression in *The Ascent of Mount Carmel,* it maintains that the encounter with God is really a journey toward encounter, a journey characterized by a certain darkness, and one which entails the progressive surrender of assuring images, concepts, feelings, which we must leave behind not because they are evil but because they are not God. "We are not he," the creatures call back to our inquiry; at the point at which we would stop the journey, the creature becomes an idol, the value becomes a disvalue, and we are no longer walking by faith.

But if this negative theology and this spiritual tradition of the dark night can help to purify, and thereby to preserve, whatever is valid in the theology and spirituality of encounter, they will not succeed in doing so unless they find formulations more congenial to contemporary Christian experience than we find in St. Thomas, St. Augustine or St. John of the Cross. The formulations must, of course, emerge from the experience of some Christians that they may in turn guide the further experience of all Christians. I do not know what the formulations might be, but I now propose, still circling around this theme, to suggest some, at least, of the ingredients of the experience itself.

The first ingredient is very aptly expressed in a statement of the French Dominican, Dominique Dubarle, "Modern humanity . . . [is] going through nothing else but a . . . democratization . . . of that night of the spirit mentioned by [St. John of the Cross]."[14] What Pere Dubarle is suggesting, I think, is that we are to look for the verification of the dark night not merely to the formal contemplation of a privileged few, but to the integral Christian experience of the entire people of God. In this period of cultural breakdown and transition, it is not only prayer forms which must be relinquished at God's call; it is a whole complexus of now unviable expressions of the Christian faith: institutional, liturgical, devotional, existential. Nor is it a question merely of substituting one set of such expressions for another. The evolutionary dimension of human life, the mobility, relativity and atomized character of man's life today, means that we have to accept living with fewer forms, especially fixed ones, in our journey toward God. This means walking for the most part in the dark, not quite sure just where we are going—it means the democratization of the dark night.

And so a good part of that asceticism of faith which is both a necessary condition for progress in prayer and the fruit of such progress will consist, for us today, in a simple willingness to live in a world and in a Church which are undergoing a cultural and institutional breaking down. One of the great enemies of true prayer is anxiety, basic anxiety, I mean— that unwillingness to let things be as they are, that "they can't do this to me" attitude. I am not suggesting here quietism or stoicism in the face of evils in Church or world, or a blunting of sensibility as the many human things we have come to love are torn from us. Rather I am speaking of a certain buoyancy, a persevering zest for life, a willingness to let things be as they are (at least as the given, as the starting point), a certain patience and withstanding of pressures (akin to the Pauline *hypomone)* especially the pressures of ever threatening despair, as we both press forward to the goal and wait for the Lord:

> Young men may grow tired and weary, youth may stumble,
>   but those who wait for the Lord renew their strength,
> They put out wings like eagles
> They run and do not grow weary
>   Walk and never tire   (Is 40:30f)

A second element in that journey of faith in the dark night where a qualified encounter with God and Christ takes place concerns the *tone* of our sacramentality. It will be, I think, a sacramentality that is more person-centered and less nature- or cosmos-centered. Liturgically it will be clearer that the sacramental sign is not the water or the oil or the wafer but the human gesture, the address of one person to another: I baptize you—I forgive you in the name of Father, Son and Spirit, I take you for better or worse, etc. Extra-liturgically, we will have to accept that the fraternity with nature in the cosmic sense of a Francis of Assisi can no longer be ours. Though communion with nature in its relatively untouched (and unblemished) state will probably always have a place in our lives this will be only a kind of counterpoint to the more basic finding of God as we may within the human city, where God manifests himself in a world worked on by human creativity of a distinctively urban style.

A third ingredient of a contemporary Christian experience which is a faith-encounter with God I would like to sum up in the phrase: *pati humana*—to be receptive to, and to be vulnerable by, fearless exposure to human life in its integrity. One of the traditional terms used to describe the purifying mystical experience is *pati divina:* to be receptive to, and vulnerable by, the searing and purifying presence of the living God. Today, it seems to me, there is need to give prominence to what was always implicit in Christian spirituality, namely that the journey of faith in the dark night is not only a plunge into the mystery of God but a descent into our humanity, a willingness to be human among humans. It is here, I think, that we modern Christians are being called to give a distinctively new expression to the imitation of Christ, to discipleship.

I would see a double aspect of this stance of *pati humana* as characteristic of Jesus and of his disciples. The first aspect is expressed by the beautiful statement of Paul: "The Son of God, the Christ Jesus that we proclaimed among you . . . was never Yes and No: with him it was always Yes, and however many the promises God made, the Yes to them all is in him. That is why it is 'through him' that we answer Amen to the praise of God" (2 Cor 1:19-20). Jesus as the man of unswerving affirmation, the perfectly responsive person, the man who always went to meet life, who always said Yes to life, most profoundly to that life which came to him from the Father—"I do always the things that please him"—but also to whatever came his way from his sinful fellow men. "I have compassion on the crowd." To be willing to let both God and man shape our destiny—*pati divina and pati humana*—this is the Yes—always Yes—to which we are called.

The second aspect of this *pati humana* is what Jesus did—and what we must do—when life does not respond to our Yes with a Yes. The author of Hebrews tells us how Jesus stood under the No—the surd of untruth and ungoodness—present in human life. He "endured a cross, despising the shame." Endurance—*hypomone*—standing up to adversity by what we may best call vulnerability—an availability for the other—for the Father and for men—that perseveres in the midst of adversity.

I will return in a moment to a more practical description of how this *pati humana* can enter into our Christian experience of praying always or finding God in all things. But first I must mention the last ingredient of a truly contemporary Christian experience, and perhaps it is the most crucial of all, and the most difficult. Its most radical expression is the saying of Jesus on which one of the statements I quoted from Bonhoeffer was based: "If you bring your gift to the altar, and there remember that your brother has something against you, go first and be reconciled to your brother—then (only then)

come and offer your gift (Mt 5:23-24). Our most basic problem
in persevering in prayer today is not that there are "death of
God" philosophers or theologians, or that science has called
in question whether God intervenes in human life or that
we are in a period of profound cultural transition. No—it is
because our brother has something against us, because, outside
of prayer, outside of liturgy, we are unreconciled and not fully
converted to Christ. And so to each one of you, and to myself
especially, in our anxiety over not praying as we should, I say:
our brother, our sister, is crying out against us, from the ghetto,
from the hamlets devastated by war, but also, less dramatically,
perhaps, but no less really, from the infirmary of our convent
or religious house, from the desks where our young students
sit, from the other end of the dining room table in our subur-
ban home. I realize that one can oversimplify. I realize that
prayer makes such reconciliation of brothers possible, as well
as being made possible by reconciliation. I appreciate that life
in the ghetto, or direct participation in the peace movement, is
not for all, and that there are many undramatic and humble
ways of engaging in the unending task of reconciliation. Still, as
an accent, as an opening out to the call for continual conversion,
we have to allow ourselves to realize over and over again that
our brothers and sisters have something against us.

The last thing I would like to do in pursuing this theme
of the possibility of an encounter with God in the conditions
of contemporary life is to describe what I feel is the ideal to
which we are tending as men and women of prayer in the
world of today. The traditional expression of this ideal is finding God in all things, praying always, habitual prayer, contemplation in action, etc. I would describe it as a *response* to value in
each human situation, and I would set it in contrast to merely
reacting to situations from instinct, prejudice or habits which
represent nature and not person. The man or woman of prayer
will be the one who, habitually, in the little, the big and the
middle-sized moments of life, will be able to say Yes, the particular Yes which the situation may demand, while resisting
and even transforming the particular No which that same

situation contains; the one who remains in the vulnerability of faith and hope, who will not seek to crawl back into the security of the womb or employ any of the myriad of artifices and evasions of which we are all such past masters; the one whose response to the situation will not proceed from mere instinct of nature, but from personal freedom, a response given *from* the Spirit, the inner dialogue-partner, and from the charity which he pours forth in our hearts, and a response which is addresseed *to* the Spirit, present in the situation itself, and especially in other human beings. Traditional theology speaks of what I am talking about in terms of the progressive return of Christian man to the state of integrity, his progressive liberation from concupiscence, from the flesh in the Pauline sense, from selfishness.[15]

Much more could be said by way of general description, but let me now particularize and illustrate. Can we be men and women of prayer in the *little* moments of life? There are a million and one little situations in life, and it is the man or woman of prayer, the responder, the Yes-sayer, the vulnerable one, who is able to assimilate and share the riches that every moment of human life contains. Watching television, for example: making the most of the commercials, whether it be the girl in the bikini, the plea to help the tiger keep his job, the tasteless shaving cream ad, and so on. Or take the experience of driving, not only the exhilaration of the superhighway but the stop and go experience of the Long Island Expressway. Or the missed connection. The broken tooth. That morning "blah" feeling. The lost ticket. The burp that escapes you at that important cocktail party. The sticky and smelly summer subway ride. The broken shoelace. But take not only the hard things, the disappointing things, the discouraging things. Take the sudden exposure to the beauty of a person, from seven to seventy; the unexpected and undeserved expression of esteem or love; the gentleness of the strong; the silent sympathy of strangers when you are embarrassed; the gift of an ordinary sunset.

There are also the larger situations: the moment you finally come to terms with the fact that you are married to an alcoholic; the phone call from your neighbor reporting that there is a black family "trying to bust our block"; the day you realize that you are forty or fifty or sixty; the day you are told you have cancer; the day you realize that you are finished as a teacher, or a surgeon, or a pastor. Or the day when the secondary supports of your priestly or religious or marital vocation suddenly collapse, and you ask yourself if there are not really other options open to you. The morning the encyclical on birth control came out, or the day you were asked to sign a protest against it.

In all such situations, small, large or middle-sized, we either respond or react, though most frequently there is something of both. But to the degree that we are men and women of prayer, the element of true response, of letting the Spirit speak through us to the situation and through the situation to us, we will be predominant. And progress in prayer means reacting less and responding more, and enjoying it more.

Those of you who are familiar with the work and philosophy of Monsignor Robert Fox in Harlem will recall his phrase of "chewing up" reality, how he speaks of "not pulling down the shades on 'the Street'." This constant moving toward reality, accepting it for better or worse, being vulnerable to it—this is what it means to pray always, to find God in all things, to be a contemplative in action. It has its difficulties, of course. It is a goal never really achieved. But it is the great adventure of life.

I suspect that we are all in agreement that this is what we are aiming at for ourselves, and especially for our young people today, even though each one would state this ideal in a different way, with different accents. So our problem of understanding prayer may not be a problem of knowing what it is, but a problem of being able to describe and relate the conditions which make it possible, for this individual or this group, in a given situation of human and Christian life, and within the limitations, opportunities and atmosphere characteristic of today's world. Among the many conditions of genuine prayer at all times, we should not forget the importance of *conversion*. I mean not only that continuing conversion (which is not so much an event as a permanent posture, more or less the vulnerability I have spoken of), but conversion as an event, no more than once or twice in a whole lifetime. I mean those rare and privileged moments when God gives us the grace to realize that we cannot live without him, and that we achieve our humanness to the degree that we live with him, and with one another in him.

Notes

[1] Dag Hammarskjöld, *Markings* (New York, 1965), p. 122. To which a *New York Times* reviewer responded, sagely, that it was also true that today the road to action necessarily passes through the world of holiness.

[2] Soren Kierkegaard.

[3] John Henry Newman, *Apologia Pro Vita Sua* (London, 1888), p. 4. The original version had "supreme" in place of "absolute."

[4] Augustine, *Soliloquies*, Book 1, Ch. 2, in *Fathers of the Church*, I (New York, 1948), p. 350.

[5] St. Augustine, *Confessions*, Book 10, Ch. 6, trans. F. Sheed (New York, 1943), p. 216.

[6] Dietrich Bonhoeffer, *The Cost of Discipleship* (New York, 1963), pp. 106-113 *passim*.

[7] *Ibid.*, pp. 144f.

[8] Dietrich Bonhoeffer, *Letters and Papers from Prison* (New York, 1962), pp. 165f.

[9] *Ibid.*, p. 219.

[10] *Ibid.*

[11] *Ibid.*, p. 175.

[12] Teilhard de Chardin, *The Divine Milieu* (New York, 1960), p. 89.

[13] Edward Schillebeeckx, *Christ the Sacrament of the Encounter with God* (New York, 1963).

[14] Quoted by C. Geffré in "Desacralization and the Spiritual Life," in *Concilium*, 19, p. 112.

[15] Cf. K. Rahner, *Theological Investigations*, I (Baltimore, 1959), pp. 347-382.

prayer and speed

-spirituality for the man of today

JEAN LECLERQ, O.S.B.

I. A NEW PROBLEM

"When you hasten hither and thither, whether you travel on foot, or do whatsoever is necessary, let your lips always ruminate some word of scripture, constantly breaking up the psalms as in a mortar, in such wise that they may ever breathe forth a perfume like that of aromatic plants."

By its faint echo of St. Paul's "we are the aroma of Christ," and by its poetry, this text strikes us as being medieval. And so it is: it dates from the eleventh century. But it is a timeless text. Written yesterday, it is actual today. From the very start it describes the modern state of things. One of its first words is the Latin *discurrere*—a verb suggesting running and quick movement. By whom was it written? And for whom? By a hermit. For a bishop. St. Peter Damian wrote it in a letter during that time of aggiornamento, updating, that historians call the Gregorian Reformation.[1] There were problems then as now: problems of prayer as well as many others.

The one which concerns us here is that of the connection between prayer, speed and noise, speed's companion. In our day, so many people travel so far, so quickly that to those of us concerned with prayer this fact raises questions: What happens to those millions of hours during which so many contemporaries scuttle to and from work or rush about for pleasure? Are they not, the more often, wasted? Could not some be recuperated, elevated, turned to profit for union with God? Does the spiritual life beat solely with nature's gentle pace, the pulsing of our body? Can it not also master modern mechanic means of motorized supersonic moving? Is recollection favored solely by stillness and slowness, and not at all by speed? Those means and methods of prayer, born before the motor age, have they still some worth? Do we have to let them drop, leave them far behind?

Those are only some of the questions confronting the modern man concerned with prayer. Who can deny that we move, are being moved, quicker and quicker, every day? The need for movement, within us, around us, is fast becoming

23

part of human nature. That is a fact which many an observer of modern man's religious conduct has noticed. Harvey Cox speaks of man's "mobility," even of his "high mobility."[2] In former days a journey was exceptional, considered as being difficult. Monastic "stability" reflected this state of things. Stability harmonized with permanence in the Lord's service according to the laws of the place where one was. Today stability has become more costly. Man is surrounded by images which "include the airport control tower, high speed elevators and perpetually moving escalators in department stores and offices. . . . Urban man is certainly in motion, and we can expect the pace and scope of mobility to increase as times goes on."[3] However, "there is no reason why Christians should deplore the accelerating mobility of the modern metropolis."[4] They must be ready to live in "a world of the jet age when the medium—speed—is the message."[5] The sheer mobility of life will also affect prayer and tend to give a new slant to thought about prayer. We live in an age when men are much less likely than ever before to settle down in any one place for any length of time."[6]

Moreover, speed is often linked with noise made by motors, agents of speed, as well as by a host of ways and means of information and expression. For example, young people often find it impossible to work without a background of pop music. This is but one aspect of the "hearing culture," the "oral-auditive" culture proper to "man in the acoustic age"—if we may recall the words used by Marshall McLuhan[7] to describe the "acoustic world" which is ours in this electronic age by reason of electrified mass media. According to McLuhan, the "hearing culture" succeeds that of the eye—of vision and reading quietly—which dates from the diffusion of printed texts. The subtitle of his second book, *Understanding Mass Media,* speaks of mass media as the *Extensions of Man.* Some of its chapters deal with the airplane, the car, telegraph, telephone, cinema, radio, television, automation. According to McLuhan, all these extensions of man are based on electric speed which, in bringing all men into almost complete communication with each other, has increased their capacity of mutual responsibility. McLuhan is concerned with the whole domain of relations between men. We will be concerned with the question of the domain of relations with God.

And so it is that motorized man—sonorized man, if we may so speak—thinks faster than his fathers: he is a "rapid thinker" thinking in a noisy world. While a child he was conditioned, psychologically and organically, to speedy reflexes; it is now a habit, and even in some countries near-hereditary. Almost instinctively man pulls the starter and steps on the accelerator at the first flicker of a green light. He hardly hears the noise of honking horns.

These are the facts of speed and sound. They can be observed today. They set a problem for those who think about prayer. Sometimes the attitude toward them is more or less one of confidence: "We live in a world of speed, images, sounds, rhythms. And the liturgy, even if it does demand dignity and coherence, does not necessarily associate piety with slowness."[8] Or else the attitude is one of skepticism as to the capacity for prayer by "modern man . . . more and more hustled and bustled because he is rationalized, collectivized, accelerated, mercilessly . . . burdened with occupations, inexorably minuted, drained by fatigue." Yet it is acknowledged that he can still find a few minutes for God "sometimes simply on his way to and from work."[9] And it is certain that this type of life scarcely prepares anyone for what is, traditionally, the cloistered, contemplative life. A monk, the Abbot S. Wicksteed, has written: "The efficiency of means of communication is gauged almost entirely by speed. But this desire for speed and more speed is radically irreconcilable with the normal rhythm of human life. There is a disastrous disproportion between the artificial febrility of modern life and the claim of nature. But modern society does not only wear itself out with haste; it wears itself out with noise as well. In the streets it is the unending roar of traffic. In the shops it is the blare of 'canned' music. In the houses it is the noise of the radio or the TV."[10]

The divergence of these opinions is due to the fact that the same question is considered from different angles by reason of varying factors, each of which must be considered independently. It is reflection on these facts and connected problems—prayer, speed, noise and humanity on the move for work or pleasure— which has suggested the following lines of research.

We have already seen that in the Middle Ages Peter Damian considered attention to God to be compatible with travel, be it gentle ambling or hasty trotting. And in our day travel is still compatible with prayer—it may even be conducive to it; further- more, it is destined to become more so. Travelling today is almost automatic. By airplane, car or subway man no longer needs to think about his mobility. The engine sees to everything; man is free to think of higher things, his inner energy is available for his spiritual, his inner life. For there is no doubt but that atten- tion to God for a passenger in an airplane is easier than it was when St. Teresa travelled in a rocking coach to help her founda- tions; easier, too, than for those who travel by boat or train in second or third class—the poor and the religious, who are God's poor. But in plane or train, although travellers may be carefree, such is not the lot of the pilot or the engineer. Unless automation has reduced him to being merely a supervisor of dials, he pays for the tranquility of the passengers with the strain made on himself. Thus speed, as everything else, is ambiguous: it can be a condition favorable to prayer, but it can also create tension and thus be an obstacle. Whatever the case, the mere fact of mov- ing, the simple sight of moving objects, is not enough for prayer. At the hub of mobility there must be some stable core; some fixed, unchanging element anchoring one to God. St. Peter Damian tells us what it is: God's word, grasped, chewed over, ruminated—in short, meditated.

This leads us to question holy scripture and tradition. Do they have anything to teach us concerning prayer allied with speed? Let us pass in rapid review the witnesses offered by holy writ, the Fathers and medieval monks. They will set us on our way, help us to probe more deeply the problems of today.

II. THE TEACHINGS OF SPIRITUAL TRADITION
Holy Writ

In the Bible, in Hebrew and in Greek, speed is expressed by words of many diverse roots. They conjure up the quality of speed: suggesting the swiftness and suddenness of an event—of death, punishment or divine intervention. Then, from the outward and physical, the meaning becomes more inward and psychical: the surface sense of "going quickly," of "acting rapidly," is connected with the troubled state aroused within the mind. Thus, the same word may signify to be agitated, excited; to be moved or afraid. Frequently, too, the material sense of "to hasten, to hurry" is spiritualized; the words depict eagerness and earnestness. We notice also that ancient Latin versions as well as the Vulgate prefer concrete terms for speed—*festinare, properare;* or *velociter, non tardare,* and still *cito, celeriter, accelerare.* Today modern translations have a liking for psychological or purely abstract connotations. In the official French translation of the breviary, for example, the word *festina,* hasten, has disappeared from the biblical verse which is recited at the start of each office. However, whatever may be the derived sense, the Bible uses speed vocabulary—apart from physical or material rapidity—to denote what we would call commitment to a cause or person. The Bible speaks of the ardor, zeal, devotedness with which one loves to serve—one does one's best, takes pains. In biblical language such notions describe man's religious attitude to events, to the ethic code, his filial piety toward God.

In the first instance, these verbal images apply to God's relations with mankind, his interventions in the coursing time of history: to the ardent expectation of the fast-approaching day when God shall manifest himself for man's salvation. Thus a psalmist sings: "He sends forth his command to the earth; his word runs swiftly" (Ps 147:15). And the prophets prophesy profoundly: God will not be long in coming, will not tarry, *non tardabit.* In consequence, man's reply to God must bear the stamp of eager swiftness. Man must know how to refrain from evildoing, to which by nature he so promptly inclines. The sapiential books give warnings. They proclaim the swiftness of God's chastizing: He who hastens to be rich will not go unpunished (Prov 28:20) ; a miserly man hastens after wealth, and does not know that want will come upon him (Prov 28:22). So it is that sacred authors tirelessly incite us to turn away from evil with all urgency, to hasten back to God: Do not delay to turn to the Lord (Eccles 5:8) .... In all your ways be quick (Eccles 31:27) .

We must avoid hasty words, rash speech, impetuosity, thoughtless haste, and yet carry out our promises with eagerness: Be not rash with your mouth, nor let your heart be hasty to utter words before God (Eccles 5:2) .... When you vow a vow to God, do not delay paying it (Eccles 5:4) ... Be not quick to anger (Eccles 7:9) cautions Coheleth, whom St. James repeats, saying, "Let every man be quick to hear, slow to speak, slow to anger" (Jas 1:19) .

This willed tardiness, born of self-control, runs hand in hand with a justified, motivated alacrity: slow for evil, quick for good —such is the friend of God. Moreover, it is hastily that God will help his friend in need. The Church turns to God at each divine hour of office. By the lips of many dedicated people— priests, monks and nuns—she cries: O Lord, make haste to help me! (Ps 69:1) . This urgent appeal has many an echo in the Bible; for example, "Incline thy ear to me, rescue me speedily!" (Ps 30:2) .

And always, at every stage of the history of salvation, we see the men and women of the Bible acting urgently: Abraham and Sarah ran, hastened to offer hospitality to the Lord (Gen 18:2, 6,7) . Rachel ran to tell her father of Jacob's coming, whereupon Laban ran to meet him (Gen 29: 12-13) . Joseph bade his brothers make haste to go up to his father (Gen 45:9) . The paschal lamb was to be eaten in all haste (Exod 12:11) . The people passed over the Jordan in haste (Jos 4:10) . In the New Testament Mary went with haste into the hill country to greet Elizabeth (Lk 1:39) . The shepherds went with haste to adore the Messiah (Lk 2:16) . Zaccheus made haste to come down from the sycamore to receive the author of his salvation (Lk 19:5) .

The father of the prodigal son ordered the servants to prepare quickly the feast of reconciliation (Lk 15:22). On Easter morning the holy women departed quickly from the tomb to announce the resurrection to the disciples and they run (Mt 28:8; Jn 20:2). Peter and John run as fast as they can toward the holy sepulchre (Jn 20:4). And after Jesus had reproached the disciples for having been "slow of heart to believe" (Lk 24:25), they went back that same hour to Jerusalem to announce the good news (Lk 24:33). Later, the Spirit told Philip to evangelize the minister of Queen Candace and Philip ran to him (Acts 8:29-30).

It is true that in Jesus himself we never notice haste, except that urgent desire to go to his baptism of blood (Lk 22:15); but this is inner ardor and desire, not outward hastiness. Jesus does everything calmly. To those who try to hold him back he says that he must preach elsewhere (Lk 4:43); yet he does not hurry to leave—he stays in each place as long as is necessary. Nor does he hasten when it is announced that Lazarus is dead (Jn 11:6) or when Herod is tracking him (Jn 11:54). One has the impression that Jesus walks in time with God. He waits for his hour to come—he anticipates nothing, precipitates nothing (Jn 2:4; 7:30; 12:27). If there is any eagerness in him, any urgency, it is that of never being distracted from his mission. One cannot help thinking, in connection with the speed of Jesus, of the words of the poet Francis Thompson: "With unhurrying chase, unperturbed pace, deliberate speed, majestic instancy."[11]

Christian eagerness is of the same mettle: it consists in hastening slowly, with all the calm of a unified life. It is multiplicity inward (that of a divided heart) or outward (that of a multitude of tasks to be done) which gives rise to haste. In the epistles of the apostles and their disciples eagerness has value as a symbol. Here we find the same note of urgency—the recurrent use of words expressing speed and swiftness—for telling of the tense seriousness of commitment to Christ, the intense ardor of Christian hope, the tension and straining forward of eschatological yearning. The Christian neither lingers nor loiters on the way to God. He presses on, strains forward, runs, runs as fast as his legs will carry him, not counting his life of any value, nor as

precious, if only he may accomplish his course (Acts 20:24).
This breathtaking eagerness, this breathless onward rush, is a
godgiven gift, a fruit of the Spirit (2 Cor 8:7, 16; 7:12).

Thus we see that speed is a human experience haloed by
the written word of God. These texts seem to suggest that in
God there is something of swiftness which, by gracious gift, he
shares with man; and that man may use this gift by serving God
swiftly or by waiting for him patiently. Time flies, we must
hasten forward to meet the Lord who comes ceaselessly toward us.

Nevertheless swiftness, as all else in sinful man, is ambiguous
and ambivalent. There is a rapidity of the sinner as well as that
of the just. Eagerness may be good or bad, just as calmness and
slowness may be the sign of either laziness or inward peace. But
more than once in the Bible, as we have seen, swiftness is considered as a positive value, and thus with optimism. As in God,
so in man, there must be all at once eagerness and patience, and
the blending of the two is characteristic of the eschatological
age of the Church: "The Lord is not slow about his promise
as some count slowness," says St. Peter, "but is forbearing toward
you, not wishing that any should perish, but that all should reach
repentance" (2 Pet 3:9). Of those whom he has visited with his
grace, God asks this alacrity, this enthusiasm, this breathless,
tireless speed—this unflagging energy by which they make a
beeline, fly toward him scorching the grass under their feet, as it
were, heedless of bystanders and onlookers. Speed is the symbol
of simplicity which hops over complications and hurdles over
complexes. Thus it is at once a sign, means and proof of that
deep union and intimacy between God and man which is the
hallmark of truly Christian prayer: simplicity is love's reply to
the Savior's secret working in a heart.

The Fathers

Among the Fathers of the Church, steeped in Bible learning
as they were, many, from Origen to the great St. Gregory, speak
of speed. For them, as for biblical writers, swiftness in relations
with God symbolizes inward energy, fervor and ardor. In this

field, as in nearly all, Origen, if we may say without quip, is the origin. For example, *The Canticle of Canticles* contains many words evoking haste: "In the odor of his sweetness, with rapid step, and all speed, they hasten."[12] In the same vein, St. Ambrose says: "Faith is swift, devotion urgent, hope quick."[13] The monk Bachiarius says: "A speedy conversion in the swiftness of repentance shall be praised."[14] "The Creator has endowed man with a mind more nimble than light, a mind able to reach out to God more swiftly than glancing eyes seize the vast immensity," says St. Augustine.[15]

God too in his dealings with man makes use of speed. We have already seen this in holy writ. The Fathers do not speak otherwise. The Son of God "deigns to accelerate the coming of his divinity."[16] His rising on the third day must be a symbol of his haste, his divine "celerity."[17] Likewise, the Lord's return, the showing forth in us of his rising from the dead, will soon be upon us. Death, resurrection and the second coming—Christ's mysteries evoking acceleration—speed onward. St. Paul, describing the rapidity with which we shall rise again, found no better comparison than the "twinkling of an eye" (1 Cor 15:52). St. Cyprian and St. Hilary exhort us to pray for the acceleration of the coming of the kingdom in order to obtain "the speed of the wondrous mercy of our God," as St. Augustine puts it.[18] Cassiodorus shows that trials and pests permitted by God "heal us swiftly, liberate us most speedily, and lead us in the way of truth."[19] Ambrose, speaking of Mary's hasty speeding into the hill country to greet Elizabeth, asks "could she do ought else but hasten to the heights, she who was full of God? The grace of the Holy Spirit does not know lagging tardiness."[20] Still another writer believes that on the day of Pentecost, the Holy Spirit appeared in the form of fire because of the quickness with which fire is communicated. Such quotations could be multiplied. They are not mere poetic phrases or facile symbolism. They translate a conviction: relations between God and man imply real speed. God intervenes swiftly for man's saving. Man must respond with alacrity at every instant. Such was the idea of the author of the Rule of St. Benedict, which supposes that from the start the candidate for monastic life desires to hurry home to heaven. The psychological implications of such a spiritual attitude have been stressed by St. Gregory the Great, who wrote the life of St. Benedict. Using the winged wheels of Ezekiel's vision—and here we cannot help but think of a Boeing upon takeoff—he compared the reader's progress in understanding Scripture to an ever-faster onward movement. Just as the living creatures Ezekiel saw seemed to be like whirling wheels, rising higher and higher, faster and faster, the divine words amplify and billow out, the reader advances.[21] The Vatican II Decree on Divine Revelation has similar words: develops, grows, constantly moves forward.

For St. Gregory the race course also symbolizes love. Peter and John raced to the tomb on Easter day; and he who loved most ran the fastest, ran on ahead, *praecucurrit*. This last word leads us to think of the precursor, John the Baptist, and all the others who, by prophetic desire, had run ahead and heralded. St. Gregory, after Origen, sees the race course as a symbol of life, but only on condition that we are billowed out, pushed forward by the breath of the Holy Spirit. Men, he says, are of different kinds: there are the motionless, the walkers, the runners, the racers. This symbolism is founded on biblical theology: "Run," says St. Paul, "run so as to carry off the prize" (1 Cor 9:24). Just as there have been precursors, so it is for us to run after him, that is, toward him: "We run after thee if we follow thee in loving thee. . . . They who contemplate God's desires, who prefer his will to theirs, run after him."[22]

For St. Gregory, as for Holy Scripture, the image of rising wheels is connected with the idea of shocks, *commotiones*. "Two big shocks give the heart emotions: one comes from fear, the other from love . . . the second comes after the whirring of wings and wheels."[23] This is desire within us; it is aroused in the Church each day as by the sound of wheels and spreading winds, by the words of Scripture and of the Fathers. By it we are able to reconcile rapidity and recollection: in silence we read, quietly; the words of life raise up the reader swiftly.

Of course, the Fathers and monks of the early Church knew

nothing of mechanical means of transport. On their travels, which were unhurried and slow, they pondered Scripture. But all that their imagination could suggest of speed—the breathless race course, whirring and rising wheels, flights—made them think of God. And, amid the milling mass of things, they perceived that musing and meditation on God's word would preserve man's unity, continuity, recollection and inward silence. It is useless to ask oneself what they would have written for our motorized age. Speed such as we know it today is full of man's ambiguity. This makes it both more sensitive and more efficacious. On the one hand the spiritual eagerness and ardor of modern man may find in the rapid means of travel a symbol and a help —they may represent the flashing presence and action of God. On the other hand this general acceleration carries with it, more and more inextricably entwined, both good and evil. But at least for the man whom grace has reconciled with self, everything furthers communion with God's Word made man in Jesus Christ.

The Middle Ages

In the Middle Ages one travelled much. And on the journey one prayed. This fact is witnessed to in many instances. In the ninth century, Prudentius, Bishop of Troyes, composed a "breviary"—an abridged psalter—for the use of a lady on her travels. In the eleventh century, St. Maiolos, Abbot of Cluny "when on horseback refreshed his mind by reading."[24] St. Peter Damian, we have seen, advised a bishop to meditate on God's word when travelling. Further examples would all have a common trait: they would show that God's word, murmured, read and meditated upon, was the stable element at the core of mobility. Furthermore, during the many processions of medieval times, the word was given back to God in proclamation; or it darted up to him in short prayers swift as arrows. These were the *saetas* or "arrow" prayers. We would call them ejaculations.

We must now ask ourselves whether spiritual masters teach anything on travelling, speed and prayer. They do. Their writings contain many allusions to these things. By way of example, let us quote just a few who have dealt more explicitly with these questions. In the eleventh century a monk of Saint Emmeran of Ratisbonne, Otloh, wrote a *Book on the Spiritual Race Course*. He starts with a quotation from St. Paul: "Do you not know that in a race all the runners compete, but only one receives the prize? So run that you may obtain it" (1 Cor 9:24). This means that we must not run behind, we have to go before, run ahead, be out in front. This race, obliging all and at all times, is desire, dogged effort. It is within the scope of all. In the stadium only the quickest and healthiest can win. But in the spiritual race, even the paralyzed can run swiftly enough. The gospel, says Otloh, gives us many lessons in speed. Everyone must hasten, each in his own way: monks and lay, pastors, ecclesiastical jurists and those who pass the time in reading scripture. The factor constant for all is God's word—food for faith, a tonic for good living. And so Otloh's treatise continues on a double plane: symbol and reality, speed and spiritual ardor.

In the twelfth century we have the example of Peter of Celle, an abbot whose style sometimes disconcerts us by its poetry. In his book *The Cloistral Discipline* he likens the cloister to a stadium; each of its dwellers may make his own the words of St. Paul: "I have fought the good fight, I have finished the race, I have kept the faith" (2 Tim 4:7). To run is to desire the goal, to strain toward it, to persevere, not to give up; it is to remain faithful. Such running supposes that we leave much behind—that we keep ourselves free from all that would weigh us down and hold us back—this is renunciation and mortification. For Peter of Celle this race is nothing less than a passing from this world to the Father, like some light runner, *cursor levis*, following on Christ's heels. The poet in Peter gives him recourse to a paschal symbolism inspired by the Fathers; he evokes the various ways of attaining the goal—by jumping, running over the fords, navigating along the mighty Euphrates.

Finally, with less exuberance but greater depth we have St. Bernard of Clairvaux. With no less charm he compares the broadcasting of the word of God to those birds which fly all the more quickly the more their wings are feathered. St. Bernard reminds us that God's "word runs swiftly" (Ps 147:15), that it was first known in Judaea alone (Ps 75:2), weighed down under the law given to Moses. Then, lightened by grace, placed upon the wheels of the gospel, it spread speedily, *velociter,* to all the earth (Ps 18:5). In his *Sermons on the Canticle of Canticles* Bernard narrates at length the way in which the word penetrates the Church—called the Bride of the Lord—and each of her members. Here we shall do no more than touch upon the theme, inspired by the words, "Draw me: we will run after thee" (Cant 1:4). Origen and Gregory the Great after him had already commented upon these words—and Bernard had certainly read their pages. First, he sketches the image of traction, drawing after; then he recalls the course which evokes eschatological desire and the fervor of love. These are gifts bestowed by him whose "word runs swiftly" (Ps 147:15), Christ, who "comes forth like a strong man to run his course" (Ps 18:6). He is God made man whom we have only to follow in his return to his Father.

> Draw me in spite of me, thus making me a willing one; draw me, a sluggard one, thus change me to a running one. The day will come when I shall need none to draw me, for willingly and with all alacrity, we will run. I will not run alone, though I alone beg to be drawn; the maidens will run with me. We will run in step, we will run together. . . . The bride has her imitators, just as she is imitator of Christ, and thus she does not say "I will run," in the singular; but, "we will run."[25]

In the rest of this sermon, St. Bernard uses the verb to run more than fifteen times. It recurs in the next sermon, where it is again linked with the incarnation which enables us to hasten on our way to God. St. Bernard shows that as soon as the Savior was born, the shepherds came in haste to adore him (Lk 2:15). "Before that, when the word was still with God, they did not move. But when he had come, they ran, they hastened."[26] Now the whole Church runs in the odor of the redemption and, within her, each one of us runs at his own speed, according to his grace. St. Bernard goes on to show that the different forms and degrees of speed are symbolized by different people in the gospel whose ardor he describes.

But speed does not symbolize only love and desire, it is also the sure sign of generous and fervent obedience: this is a constant in traditional ascetic teaching. St. Benedict, for example, insists that an order should be executed without delay. And St. Bernard, in praise of speed, gave rein to his imagination and literary genius in two texts full of quotes from the Old and New Testaments. It would not be difficult to show that, like many other representatives of spiritual tradition, he did not fail to use the vocabulary of speed when speaking of union with God at all levels of Christian living.

III.   TODAY

Today, speed is no longer merely a dream and a symbol—it is a daily fact. It is within the reach of many for their leisure hours and of many more by necessity of existence. One must move quickly—at work if the job demands; if work is sedentary one must still travel there and back. Furthermore, the effects of our age of urban civilization have spread to the countryside. Contemporaries no longer take their relaxation at home or in gentle promenading. They rush to another place by means of speeding transport. Even sports and games—traditional forms of relaxation and leisure—are giving ever greater room to speed. Even when no record is to be broken, what counts is often not the goal attained but the mere pleasure of speeding toward it. It would seem as though man's progress, his growth in self-control, consists in moving, on foot or horse, by motor or sail, or by any means he chooses; in moving faster, ever faster on the race course, on the mountain track or on the crests of waves; or in rushing pell-mell after a ball, kicking, throwing, hitting it. Yesterday slowness in decision and reluctance for change were counted virtues; today society questions such deliberateness.

We must dwell upon these facts and try to find in them some

sense for the spirituality of our times. Rapid obedience was considered a gift of the Holy Spirit. Would it not possibly be the same in prayer? Is speed conducive to prayer? Can it become more so? These questions, of course, in no way criticize "formal prayer," which stillness often favors. Here we are dealing with something else.

The Facts of Experience

Let us start by recalling some facts of spiritual experience linked with and dependent upon rapid travelling. I was told, for example, by one of the best informed men on Christian living in Paris that the subway is the place in Paris where most praying is done! He added that churches do not thereby become superfluous, for there are still people who like to stop for a moment in them. Another man, well acquainted with pastoral work and spirituality, did not hesitate to say: "The Paris subway is less 'worthy' than my church, but I am more attentive in it: the presence of the anonymous crowd calls for prayer... I say my breviary very well in the train when I have a long journey ahead."[27] The same observations could be made, of course, about other means of transport. The chief conditions conducive to prayer in public vehicles are peace of mind (one knows how long the journey will last) and the presence of an anonymous crowd which, while respecting each traveller's recollection, nevertheless stirs his mind to a sense of communion, solidarity, responsibility, and so intercession. According to one's position and the available space there is the possibility of reading or silent meditation. Since one does not have to take charge of the engine, one is entirely free to concentrate on such matters. But even the driver, alone in his cab or at his seat must often have moments, perhaps even long moments, during which he has a chance to pray. This last factor is particularly true for car drivers. Once, while travelling with a friend in California, he told me that he made a habit of singing hymns and spiritual canticles when at the wheel. This engineer in advanced electronics fitted two hours of daily prayer between his home and his laboratory. And, so he told me, when held up in traffic along-side a strained, anxious driver glaring at the red light, nervous, fidgety and impatient for the change of color, he called to him, inviting him to relax and take it easy: even when he was not praying he was an apostle of prayer. Many people whom I have questioned on this point have said that they find it easy to pray when driving their car. There are even contemplatives who long for the time when they will be on the road again for long hours and alone with God.

It would be possible to select from contemporary spiritual literature a very instructive anthology concerning the relation between prayer and travel. Saint-Exupery, we know, had a gift for associating airplane flights with admirable spiritual experiences. Nothing will be said here on the spirituality of sport, of self-surpassing by dint of discipline—this calculated, measured effort to go beyond one's limits belongs to another field of human experience. Rather than speak of such exceptional experiences, we will consider the ordinary goings from place to place. The Maritains have devoted some fine pages to this in their *Priere sur les chemins*. Father Voillaume has entitled a book *Sur les chemins de Dieu*. The texts of this latter work were nearly all written at different stages of numerous journeys; they were often inspired by men and facts observed as he travelled about. We may also recall the elevations of Malcolm Boyd's *Are You Running with Me, Jesus?* and Michel Quoist's *Prayers*. A modern mystic, Gabrielle Bossis, lived in the world and from 1936 on-ward travelled widely in Europe, North Africa, America and the Near East. Her spiritual notes have been published under the title *He and I*. All her reflections have traveller's titles: On a ship . . . In the Austerlitz station buffet . . . At Saint Lazare Station . . . In the train . . . Waiting for breakfast before leaving the hotel . . . In the bus from Kerouan to Susa . . . About travellers loaded with luggage . . . On the boulevard . . . Boulevard Raspail . . . Train terminus . . . Paray-le-monial Station. Other thoughts prompted by the movings of the Holy Spirit include: In a church . . . In my hotel room . . . In a café . . . At the dentist's . . . At the theater. It is quite to be expected that the contemplative whose job it was to travel much should have prayed on her journeys. All she saw or heard led her to converse with her Lord: he spoke to her and she answered him without delay. There is little of the Bible in her writings (she wrote before the biblical renewal) but today her piety would undoubtedly have been nourished on the scriptures. Nevertheless her basic psychological attitude facilitates presences to God in every circumstance, especially when travelling. It is a simple and constant attention which is stimulated and aroused by the slightest happening; it blossoms out in an act of prayer, a raising of the mind and heart to God. Such travelling contemplatives are oases of solitary prayer in the unheeding, seething crowd.

Many of those whom monastic tradition venerates as God's saints took to the road in order to find him in the solitude of exile, in the asceticism and inward recollection of pilgrim wandering. This practice still has its devotees. Discretion forbids me to say much, but one of them confided this to me: "When I have spent three hours in adoration in church, then I pray best when walking in town." Another contemplative from a convent in the Near East told me of the deep recollection that was hers when, leaving the convent, she was lost in the seething oriental crowd. As for prayer in planes, one has only to try to see how well one prays. It is possible to be a hermit in the skies for a whole day and more, alone with God for long hours on end, at one's seat or in airport corridors, amid the anonymous crowd of brother travellers whose presence is a stimulant to charity. Travelling can create a state of mind compatible with prayer; in some it may even give rise to singularly elevated spiritual gifts. Swift travel is both a sign and a means of communication, of possible communion and of detachment—of charity in many forms.

Certain reflections on the facility of prayer in an anonymous crowd also point out why prayer is experienced as being difficult when neither place nor persons vary, when the milieu is always the same. The psychological connection between the activity of prayer and environment is ambiguous: helpful to some, a hindrance for others. Variation and anonymity of milieu may just as easily impede as further real charity, which commits us to the persons with whom we live and are in daily contact.

The psychic state resulting from travel should not resemble that produced by some narcotics. There are people who are greatly inspired by the influences around them. Furthermore, if change in the organism and its outer milieu does liberate the unconscious and help it to express itself, it is often at the expense of voluntary consciousness. We need only think of whirling dervishes. In the domain of acceleration all depends on each one's grace and the mastery which he keeps over himself. But at least we may affirm that prayer is not necessarily tied down to sometimes artificial conditions of solitude and immobility to which it has sometimes been too narrowly connected.

Finally, bound up with the problem of mobility, there is noise. Diffused, continuous street noise is no longer considered a source of distraction. For certain people it has come to be a background noise indispensable for concentration and prayerful activity: today we even have liturgical music composed to the sounds of the street. We have learned to admire the countryside against such background noise: from airports, from missile launching stations and from railroad depots. Today there is an effort being made to bring noise down to a minimum, to avoid sudden, sharp and startling sounds. Noise, therefore, tends to become soft and gentle, purring and whirring, which in no way distracts the willing mind from God. In other religions, loud noise is often conditional and expressive of a spiritual attitude. In India, "even within the temple walls the noise is deafening and the hammering of big drums has something terrifying about it, and, if we are not too stunned by the racket to pay attention, we are stupefied to notice that there are some who seem to find this atmosphere of row and noise particularly propitious to reading, study, meditation, prayer and everything that requires recollection, withdrawal into self and inner silence."[28] Another example of different forms of asceticism and prayer which makes use of mobility is offered by the dervishes and wandering hermits of Islam and Hinduism.

To conclude this short survey of data offered by modern

witnesses in favor of prayer accompanied with speed and noise, let us quote Harvey Cox once again: "People on the move spatially are usually on the move intellectually, financially or psychologically."[29] Experience seems to allow us to add "spiritually." There is no longer any doubt that in the domain of the spiritual life mobility has its effect, either good or bad, conscious or unconscious. This ambivalence is a problem about which it is our duty to think in order to get the most out of mobility in favor of union with God.

Toward a Spirituality of Speed

We have seen that speed may help or hinder man on his way to God. It all depends on the use to which it is put. Travelling makes prayer more difficult because the journey obliges us to leave our habitual environment and break with routine: prayer ceases to be habit; it must be willed, voluntarily assumed. Travel obliges us to take the initiative if we want to raise our mind and heart to God. Yet, on the other hand, a journey facilitates prayer. Though we have to will to pray in the train, car or plane, our faculties, set free from absorbing occupations, are ready for union with God. Even for a man whose job it is to travel the conditions are often favorable. The pilot of a plane, for example, knows that at the least sign of danger, a warning signal will light up before his eyes. This allows him to relax, to settle down; his mind is free, available for prayer if he so desires. It is not for us to make a psychological analysis of these secondary factors favoring relaxation, but we all know by daily experience that they are real, positive factors. Obviously we must be realists—speed is not always conducive to prayer—the driver of a race car is certainly not disposed to prayer when on the race course; the driver of a harvester will have more of a chance.

The motor age has aroused new problems for the religious conscience—factors about which our ancestors never even dreamed. Pius XII and his successors have often reminded car drivers that they have no right to endanger the lives of others by reckless driving. Writers such as H. Renard in his *L'auto-mobiliste et la morale cretienne,* have enlarged upon the practical consequences of this obligation. A widely read Catholic Truth Society pamphlet has the title *May I Drive as I Please?* Its aims are described in the subtitle, "The Code of the Road and Ethics." The pamphlet contains an article by Bishop Janssens which appeared first in a most serious theological journal. For those who travel by Olympic Air Lines, the welcoming words, *Hail, Stranger (Kaire Xene)* remind him of the *xenitheia,* a form of asceticism and prayer practiced by the first monks and Fathers of the Church. It implied departure for voluntary exile: detachment, risk—and hope. Today, as then, many a man is a solitary traveller, lost in the crowd of anonymous fellow travellers which chance brings across his path, beside whom he is seated for a short while in public conveyances and with whom he shares destinies for a brief moment in time. This solidarity with travelling crowds does not necessarily involve the solitary in gregariousness: provided he retains his inner liberty, he is *in* the crowd, but not *of* the crowd. And the loneliness of this solitary prayer may even give rise to a fresh appreciation, call up new possibilities of real communion with the Christian assembly. Jesus sometimes withdrew into himself in order to pray while in company with his disciples. St. Luke tells us "Now it happened that as he was praying alone the disciples were with him" (Lk 9:15). At other times Jesus withdrew to a lonely place apart, went into the hills to pray. Sometimes he prayed aloud in their presence, with them and for them. Thus he left us an example showing that we may be with God even though among men. From the earliest times to our day, Christ has always had disciples to follow in his footsteps. Times and people have greatly changed since the days when Christ walked the earth; but prayer when travelling, be it by road, sea or air, has remained a constant. As was suggested at the start of this paper, the word of God has always been the stable element which allows this itinerant prayer; it is the word of God which amid the chances and changes of space and time, "remains forever" (Is 40:8). "To remain": a theme cherished by St. John and my monastic tradition; to remain is to be fixed in union by love. He who loves, wherever he goes, whatever he does, is turned toward the loved one; his thoughts wander back instinctively to the object of his love each time that his attention ceases to be absorbed by some other task. Prayer is an expression of love; prayer is faithful in the measure that love is faithful. What better proof of love is there than to repeat and ruminate the words of the loved one, to translate them, faithfully, lovingly, and eagerly in daily life? Is it surprising that men and women of prayer have always liked to muse over God's word, to think upon a word of holy scripture? In connection with this type of prayer, the medieval spiritual writers did not hesitate to use terms like chewing, ruminating. As odd and unbecoming as it may seem, this idea is best translated in modern language by comparing the word of God to chewing gum, or to a sweet which is sucked. This idea will not shock us if we remember that St Francis de Sales and Claudel, two great poets of prayer, did not hesitate to use the language of their day in connection with prayer. What counts is to grasp the idea behind the words—the idea expressed by St. Peter Damian in the text quoted at the beginning. Continuous prayer during journeys supposes that the word of God is rooted in the traveller's mind and heart, and that it is given back to God spontaneously at all times. This explains why the ancients had a preference for short, pithy phrases, brief invocations, the Jesus Prayer, which were easy to memorize and easily recalled.

Naturally, this requires some education; it does not come from the simple fact of being in a state of grace; of having faith, hope and charity; it does not set off automatically at fixed intervals. Such prayer presupposes preparation. For the word of God to be graven in the memory, it must first have been read, heard and sung many times. Furthermore, one must have sufficient control of mind and body to remain attentive to God, to swivel back to him like the compass needle coming to rest in the direction of the magnetic north. The least event stimulates attention to God—the slightest happening (as was often the case for Gabrielle Bossis) calls forth a spiritual reaction. Everything becomes a sign evoking a word. But this word must be already hidden within the heart, waiting for the first occasion to change into prayer. If so few people today are able to respond prayerfully to the stimulus of rapid movement and made good use of psychic relaxation which high speed travelling and solidarity with their fellow travellers favors, it is perhaps because they have not yet learned to master either themselves or the mobility of their environment. They are not yet adapted to this high-speed spirituality. But a deeper reason may be that they never learned to make use of environmental conditions for prayer. Much remains to be done both in the education, or reeducation of modern man and in the updating of spiritual concepts and practices. New end-concepts must be introduced into religious psychology and they must be connected with the notion of situation. The new spiritual man will be the one who commands the new travel situation, the one who masters speed, mobility and noise, making them agents of his inner peace and union with God.

This, of course, in no way diminishes the possible value of immobility. An alternating of traditional forms of recollection with new forms remains desirable. We must, however, have confidence in mobility and rapidity as authentic means of union with God. The recovery for prayer of the countless hours spent daily in travelling is a complex one involving psychology, spirituality and mechanics. The mysterious activity called prayer has always been considered as time spent for God alone. And this fact of tradition must be maintained. But what is the nature of the time to be given? How must it be given? Slowly? Rapidly? In mobility or immobility? With or without background noise? There are many possibilities. Experience alone will tell what is suitable for each one of us. We have seen that the word *accelerare* occurs more than once in the Bible. The theology of acceleration, the ethics for the accelerator, cannot ignore the precise notion of what is meant by acceleration in mechanics and the repercussion it has on human behavior. A continuous movement does not disturb the organism, no matter how rapid it may be. It is the sudden change of speed which gives the organism a shock, as when an elevator starts or stops, or when a plane touches down or takes to the air. But for many of us, measured, calculated, foreseen, controlled speed, safeguarded by a brake, favors relaxation. For man, then, to be submitted to rapidity, or rather, to submit it to his liberty, is not an obstacle to his capacity for prayer. "In the clouds to meet the Lord in the air" (1 Thess 4:17). We may recall these words of St. Paul with a smile when we take a plane. Does it not remind us of that "agility" which, so theologians tell us, will be one of the "gifts" of our glorified bodies?

Notes

[1] "Inédits de S. Pierre Damien," in *Revue bénédictine,* 67 (1967), p. 158.

[2] Harvey Cox, *The Secular City* (New York, 1966) pp. 43-44.

[3] *Ibid.,* p. 45.

[4] *Ibid.,* p. 51.

[5] John B. Coburn, "The Chairman's Introduction to the Conference," in *Spirituality for Today, Papers from the 1967 Parish and People Conference,* ed. Eric James (London, 1968), p. 57.

[6] Douglas Rhyner, *Prayer in the Secular City* (London, 1967), p. 17.

[7] Cf. *The Gutenberg Galaxy* (University of Toronto Press) and *Understanding Mass Media: Extensions of Man* (New York, 1966).

[8] R. Gregoire, O.S.B., "Epilogo sull' evoluzione della liturgia," in *Ora et Labora,* 23 (1968) p. 85.

[9] J. Mouroux, "La prière et le temps," in *Bulletin du Cercle S. Jean-Baptiste,* 26 (December, 1963), pp. 17-18.

[10] Abbot S. Wicksteed, "Religious and the Young Church," in *Spode House Review* 3 (1967), p. 18.

[11] "The Hound of Heaven."

[12] *In Cant. cant.,* 1, I, ed. Baehrens (Leipzig, 1925), p. 102.

[13] 97, *P.L.,* 16, 1215.

[14] "De reparatione lapsi," 4, *P.L.,* 20, 1040.

[15] St. Augustine, *De Gen. ad litt.,* 4, 34, CSEL, 28, 1, p. 135.

[16] *Panegyrici,* 5, 13, ed. Baehrens (1874).

[17] Cassiodorus, *In Act.,* 16, 38, *P.L.,* 70, 1395.

[18] *Conf.,* 9, 4, 12, CSEL, 23, p. 206.

[19] Cassiodorus, *In Ps. 31,* 10 CCL 97, p. 281.

[20] *In Luc.,* 2, 19, CCL 14, p. 39.

[21] *In Ez.,* I, 78, *P.L.,* 843-844.

[22] *In Cant.,* 1, 10, *P.L.,* 79, 482.

[23] *In Ez.,* I, 39, *P.L.,* 76, 902.

[24] Syrus, *Vita Maioli*, III, 3, MG, SS, 1V.

[25] *Sup. Cant.*, 21, 9, ed. *S. Bernardi opera*, I Rome, 1957, p. 127.

[26] *Ibid.*, 22, 5, p. 132.

[27] H. Le Sourd, P.S.S. "Un cure de paroisse et son breviare," in *La Maison-Dieu*, 64 (1960), p. 123.

[28] A. Desjardin, *L'hindouisme et nous* (Paris, 1964), p. 60.

[29] Cox, *op. cit.*, p. 46.

contemplation of the gospels and the contemporary christian

DAVID M. STANLEY, S.J.

T he question to which we address ourselves[1] is of particular
concern to those who give or make the Spiritual Exercises of
St. Ignatius Loyola in our age. Yet, I venture to suggest, it is a
problem of more general, if not universal interest to any twentieth-century Christian, conscious of the profound differences
separating his own world view from that of the evangelists, or,
for that matter, from the *Weltanschaung* of medieval and
renaissance man. The Christian of today feels compelled to ask
the very relevant question, "Why contemplate the earthly history
of Jesus of Nazareth?"

Modern man experiences real difficulty when asked to recall
scenes from a life lived twenty centuries ago, in cultural and
historical circumstances foreign to himself, his problems, the
world in which he finds himself. At best such a spiritual exercise
appears to be an effort of the devout memory or of the pious
imagination. Not a few Christians, who have attempted to make
the Spiritual Exercises have found the experience baffling,
uncongenial, ineffectual. It has seemed to them a laborious
attempt to situate the "imitation of Christ" (presented all too
often in a quite moralistic fashion) in the original context of
Jesus' own earthly existence. The frustrating struggle to re-
construct the past in this way may well appear to the intelligent,
twentieth-century exercitant—even where the history of Jesus
is concerned—an exercise in futility. How is it profitable, necessary, or even possible?

Why not as well consider the life of Socrates presented to
us in the dialogues of Plato? The query is not altogether cynical
or irrelevant. The virtues and nobility of character exhibited by
that great philosopher are for the most part worthy of "imitation" by any Christian; and the literary presentation of Plato is
undoubtedly superior in many respects to the writing of Mark
or Matthew, even of John or Luke. We shall return presently
to this question of the life of Socrates, as it will help our comprehension of the value of contemplating the Gospel narratives.

Actually, the question we are considering is a twofold one,
and requires a twofold answer. In the first place, there is the very
basic problem: what benefit can accrue to the Christian of today

from the contemplation of the mysteries of Jesus' earthly life, when the Christ who exists now is none other than the exalted Lord? Secondly, why should the Gospel accounts of Jesus' public ministry and his earthly career—even granting their inspired character—be deemed a *locus privilegiatus* through which the modern believer can enjoy a genuine religious experience, and so be led to enter a deeper personal relationship with the *Kyrios*, to whom he has already by faith and baptism committed himself and his life?

To appreciate the difficulty which the modern mentality frequently feels in attempting to make the Spiritual Exercises of St. Ignatius, it will help to recall certain characteristics of that medieval piety, seemingly congenial in large measure to the author of the *Spiritual Exercises*, which are alien to the man of today. The point is of some significance, since, if the *Spiritual Exercises* are to have the desired impact upon the twentieth-century man of the Church, particularly upon the post-conciliar Catholic mind, it is crucial that such an exercitant be given an understanding of the purpose, an appreciation of the value of the Ignation contemplation. For this it is necessary that this method of prayer, so characteristic of Ignatian spirituality, be presented without those vestigial remnants of medieval piety occasionally discernible in the text of the *Spiritual Exercises*.[2]

Medieval man was gifted with a highly developed imagination, since he was, broadly speaking, the product of a culture which antedated the invention of printing. Medieval Christians contemplated the mysteries of faith as they found them portrayed in the sculpture, stained glass, frescoes, even the architecture of the great shrines and cathedrals which surrounded them. These "bibles" of the common people depicted the earthly history of Jesus replete with many details not found in the austere, somewhat jejune accounts of the Gospels. The Middle Ages did, of course, produce lives of Christ like that of Ludolph the Carthusian, which fed the imagination as well as the piety of the converted Inigo de Loyola. In consequence, medieval piety may be fairly described as largely engrossed with the "historical details" (all or most of them the creation of fertile, if pious, imaginations) of Jesus' earthly life. One thinks immediately of the Christmas crib, the contribution of a St. Francis of Assisi, or of those revelations of the Passion, replete with such gruesome details, found in writings like those of St. Bridget of Sweden. This same spirit is to a degree discernible in St. Ignatius himself, who gladly bribed his Muslim guide to permit him a second look at the stone on the Mount of Olives, said to bear the imprint of the foot of the ascending Christ.

Nor is the little book of the *Spiritual Exercises* entirely free from the creative ingenuity which characterized medieval piety. In the contemplation on the Incarnation, the exercitant is bid attend to "what the three divine Persons are saying, viz: 'Let us work out the redemption of the human race ...'" (107) [3] Likewise, there is the gratuitious introduction of "a servant-girl" into the contemplation of the Nativity (111,114). Here, in addition, the retreatant is asked to "account myself a poor and unworthy servant, looking at and contemplating them and tending them in their necessities as though I were present there ..." (114). There is also the reference to the Magi as "the three kings" (162), a legendary development not found in the Gospel text. There is, finally, the familiar directive, recurring like a refrain in so many second preludes, which encourages the free use of the imagination with regard to "the road from Nazareth to Bethlehem" (112), "the supper room" (192), "the arrangements of the holy sepulchre, and the place or house of our Lady" (220).

All of this, as I have said, is alien, if not distasteful to our modern mentality. I believe it may be said that our present-day respect for the biblical narratives themselves and our concern to grasp the intention of the evangelists in presenting Jesus' earthly history as they do, make it impossible, indeed undesirable, for us to attempt to carry out *ad litteram* the instructions of St. Ignatius in our contemplations of the Gospel scenes. More important still, the injunctions of the *magisterium* of the Church not only permit but encourage this procedure. Some twenty-five years ago Pius XII in *Divino afflante Spiritu* directed our attention to the text of Scripture, and especially to the discovery of its literal sense, which he called "the genuine sense of the sacred books,"[4] while granting that "not every spiritual sense is excluded from Sacred Scripture." He insisted strongly upon recovering "what the writer meant to say" as "the supreme law of interpretation."[5] The recent conciliar Constitution on Divine Revelation, *Dei Verbum,* urged that "all, especially religious" should "gladly put themselves in touch with the sacred text itself."[6] *Perfectae Caritatis,* the decree of Vatican II on the renewal of religious life, has declared that "the fundamental norm of the religious life is a following of Christ as proposed by the gospel."[7]

Before an attempt is made to answer the questions we have proposed about the contemplation of the Gospel narratives, it may not be out of place to recall how prominently this form of prayer figures in two of the most influential documents in the history of Christian spirituality, the *Spiritual Exercises* of St. Ignatius and the *Regula Monachorum* ascribed to St. Benedict.

In the *Spiritual Exercises* the contemplation is distinguished from meditation: the meditation is an exercise proper only to the first week, while the contemplation is characteristic of the rest of the thirty days of the Exercises. Two significant exercises of the second week constitute the only exception to this latter point: the two meditations called "Two Standards" (136-148) and "Three Classes of Men" (149-157). In the mind of St. Ignatius, the meditation appears to have as its object certain realities of faith (original sin, hell, the contemporary struggle between the risen Christ and the powers of evil in "Two Standards"), which may be termed "meta-historical." The contemplation, by contrast, is orientated to the *mysteries* contained in the earthly history of Jesus. Thus in the fourth week there is no contemplation on the resurrection, but only on the post-resurrection appearances.

A certain ambiguity remains in the Ignatian distinction between meditation and contemplation. It comes as a distinct surprise to find the final exercise, in which neither Christ nor the mysteries of his earthly life are ever mentioned, denominated as the "Contemplation for attaining love" (230-237); and perhaps "contemplation" is employed here only in an analogous sense. Moreover, a certain fluidity in Ignatius' terminology is perceptible in the note to the "mysteries of the life of Christ our Lord," appended to the four weeks, which speaks of "meditating and contemplating them" (261). Whether or not any completely satisfactory solution can be given to this problem, it is clear that St. Ignatius relied mainly upon the contemplation of the earthly history of Jesus for the effectiveness of his carefully constructed program of Spiritual Exercises. This form of Christian prayer unquestionably constitutes the wellspring of Ignatian spirituality.

In the eyes of St. Benedict, *lectio divina,* the meditative reading of the Scriptures constitutes, together with manual labor and the *opus Dei* (choral recitation of the divine office), one of the principal activities of the monastic life. The conception of *lectio divina* found in the *Regula Monachorum* illustrates the traditional Christian belief in the creative dynamism of the Scriptures, among which the Gospels hold the place of honor. This important monastic exercise is understood to demand the full, active attention and cooperation of the monk. Its salient feature is presented by the significant phrase *meditare aut legere:* hence it is the prayerful reading of the Bible by the Christian. Yet it is not only or primarily an intellectual exercise, for the Bible addresses itself to the whole man, not merely to the top of his head.

"Whatever was written of old," says St. Paul, "was written for our instruction, that by patience and the *consolation* of the Scriptures we might have hope" (Rom. 15:4). "All Scripture is divinely inspired and spiritually advantageous for teaching, reproof, correcting error, formation in righteousness, so that the man of God may be equipped properly and effectively prepared for every good work" (2 Tim. 4:16-17). Accordingly, *lectio divina* is associated by St. Benedict with *compunctio cordis,* the ongoing process of *metanoia* (cf. Acts 2:37-38), which is the purpose of the Christian gospel. *Lectio divina* is aimed at producing a religious experience in the Christian reader: it has an essentially *heilsgeschichtlich* quality. In other words it is a prayerful exercise calculated to terminate in a "saving event," which is to be experienced by the Christian reader. Such a view reposes fundamentally upon the belief that the most significant kind of truth contained in the Bible is "saving truth": "the truth which God has willed to put into the sacred books for the sake of our salvation."[8]

It is interesting to observe that this ancient Benedictine practice of *lectio divina* was recently warmly recommended to the Society of Jesus by the General Congregation of that order in its decree on prayer. *"Lectio divina,* a practice dating back to the earliest days of religious life in the Church, supposes that the reader surrenders to God who is speaking and granting him a change of heart under the action of the two-edged sword of scripture continually challenging to conversion."[9]

In the first part of this study we shall seek to discover what basis there is in reality for the Ignatian and Benedictine conviction that the contemplation of the mysteries of Jesus' earthly history in the gospel narratives is not only possible but highly efficacious for the Christian of any era. We shall do this chiefly by examining the implications contained in an ancient credal formula which has come down to us from the apostolic age. In a second part of this essay we shall attempt to explain how this contemplation of the gospels can be successfully carried out, how it may be considered to result in a truly "saving event".

I. "JESUS IS LORD!"

A Christian may be quite simply described (as Karl Rahner has somewhere asserted) as a man who has accepted Christ. To borrow from the language of modern psychology, the Christian —to be a Christian and not merely bear the name—must be able to "relate to" Jesus Christ. To be meaningful and operative in his Christian existence, his act of faith must be a whole-hearted commitment of his total self to the Lord Jesus. Faith is the *engagement* of the whole man to the person of Christ: it is nothing if it is not actually a profound interpersonal relationship with him who through death and resurrection has acceded to universal power as the Master of history, the Lord of the universe.

This was, beyond any doubt, the conviction of the first-century Christians whose faith we in the twentieth century claim to share. These first disciples expressed their paschal faith through a formula that remains at once the most primitive and most concise *credo* which has come down to us: *lēsous Kyrios!* (Jesus is Lord!) In a highly imaginative, yet deeply theological manner, the unknown author of a liturgical hymn,[10] cited by Paul in writing to the Philippians, presents the collaboration of all creatures in the divine work of the redemption as a kind of cosmic liturgy:

> "Therefore did God in turn immeasurably exalt him,
> and graciously bestow on him the Name
> outweighing every other name:
>
> that everyone at Jesus' Name[11]
> should bow adoring: those in heaven,
> on earth, in the infernal regions;
>
> and every tongue take up the cry,
> 'Jesus is Lord!'—
> thus glorifying God his Father."   (Phil. 2:9-11)

This hymn, of Palestinian origin, was probably familiar to the Philippian community from the celebration of the Eucharistic liturgy. It witnesses to the fact that the understanding of the cosmic proportions of Jesus' Lordship was already part of apostolic tradition. It also reveals how important this article of faith was for the significance of the liturgy of the Church. The central act of Christian worship, where the Church is most consciously herself, is the acknowledgment that "Jesus is Lord!" It is moreover her awareness of this article of faith that distinguishes the Church from "the world," which does not know that Jesus is Lord; and so gives the Church her sense of mission in history, to proclaim this salutary truth in the gospel.

Paul reminds the Corinthian community that this act of

faith can only be made with the assistance of the Holy Spirit. "No one can say 'Jesus is Lord!' except through the influence of the Holy Spirit" (1 Cor 12:3). In fact, this brief creed sums up, for Paul, the essential message of the apostolic kerygma, and defines the role of those to whom the ministry of preaching is confided by the Church. "For we do not proclaim ourselves, but Jesus Christ as Lord, and ourselves as your slaves with respect to Jesus" (2 Cor 4:5).

In writing to the Roman church Paul insists upon the necessity for salvation of the public profession of this little formula, which epitomizes Christian belief. "For if you confess with your mouth 'Jesus is Lord!,' and you believe in your innermost self that God raised him from death, you will be saved" (Rom 10:9). Somewhat later, Paul will declare to the Colossians that this formulation of Christian belief provides the pattern for Christian living, reminding them of its traditional character. "Therefore, since you have accepted the Messiah Jesus as Lord from tradition, live your lives in union with him" (Col 2:6). This last statement is of particular interest to us here, inasmuch as it indicates how profoundly this conception of the exalted Christ influenced the attitudes of the apostolic Church. Accordingly, it is necessary to reflect upon the various dimensions of meaning it contained for the first Christians.

It is sometimes stated that the primitive Christians were completely obsessed with the expectation of Jesus' second coming, an event moreover which they (erroneously as the passing of two thousand years have shown) thought to be imminent. While it must be granted that the expectation of a proximate parousia figured prominently in the thinking of the apostolic age, the fact remains that these first and second generation Christians displayed, on the evidence of the formula of faith which we have just considered, a greater and more absorbing interest: the serene preoccupation with the *contemporary Christ,* who, they firmly believed, as Lord of history effectively directed the destinies of his Church as well as of the entire universe. The significance of this central tenet of the faith of the apostolic Church lies in her confident and optimistic conviction that Jesus

Christ through his exaltation to the Father's right hand has *not* been removed to some mythical existence beyond the furthest galaxy, but is *actually more dynamically present* in the world than ever he was when he walked the hills of Galilee. Far from implying a withdrawal from the contemporary scene or a shadowy evanescence in the mists of some mythical apotheosis, Jesus' ascension meant to the early Church a mysterious, invisible, but nonetheless real and powerful reentry into the ongoing historical process. This is the most fundamental meaning of the ancient formula of faith, "Jesus is Lord!"

This unshakable belief of the apostolic Church explains a noteworthy feature of the entire New Testament, an outlook particularly prominent in the theological attitude of the four evangelists. Search as you will, you will discover in their books no nostalgia for "the good old days." As a result of the coming of the Holy Spirit, Jesus' first disciples had no desire, made no attempt to live in the past, or to turn back the clock by wishing to return to the privileged intimacy with Jesus, which they had enjoyed during the years of his public ministry. Their newly given Christian faith directed their attention toward the glorified Lord Jesus, who now stood revealed to them as the very incarnation of *aggiornamento,* forever up-to-date, continually abreast of the happenings of this world. Indeed, as they well realized, he "went before" them (cf. Mt 28:7) constantly; and their most imperative duty was to run to catch up to him, who in glory presents the astonishing spectacle of the "the last Adam," the first-redeemed man, the last word in human perfection—and hence the final goal of redeemed humanity.

The risen Christ was in the second place, revealed to them through their paschal faith as the Son of God who had freely chosen to remain human for all eternity. He was proclaimed in the apostolic kerygma as having, through his death and resurrection, become the paragon of human perfection, the image of God in flesh and blood, the model according to which every human being must be remolded, and so made conformable. For, as Paul reminds us, it is the declared design of the Father that we "should be shaped over in the image of his Son, that he (the

Son) might become the eldest of a large family of brothers"
(Rom 8:29).

But how is this transfiguration of the Christian, this re-
modelling of humanity in the image of the risen Christ to be
effected? St. Paul, enucleating the teaching of Jesus himself,
assures us that "flesh and blood cannot inherit the kingdom of
God" (1 Cor 15:50; 6:13). Man to be redeemed must in the
totality of his person, on the material no less than on the
spiritual side, be transformed by participation in the paschal
mystery, revealed to the apostolic Church as already embodied
in the exalted Lord Jesus. This amazing truth is for Paul the
message of hope to mankind in despair of salvation, *the* mystery
divinely revealed in Jesus Christ: "we shall all be changed!" (1
Cor 15:51; 1 Thes 4:15-17). Yet such a necessary and marvelous
transformation, we are assured, does not destroy our human
nature, does not dehumanize us by dissolving the material aspect
of our personality. On the contrary, Paul confidently asserts that
the "omega point" of man's destiny, the Lord of history, who
has chosen to remain human forever, is to be found, not in
retreat from this world, but in the monotonous, daily round of
human experiences, where he confronts the Christian personally
in his own existential situation. This constitutes for Paul the
basic reason for his view that every human being must endeavor
to find Christ by persevering with constancy in his own station
in life. "I am convinced then of this, that it is a good thing
(because of the present time of stress) that a man remain as he
is" (1 Cor. 7:26). For, as a consequence of the death and resurrection of Christ, the whole of history has received a totally new
orientation; and things can never be the same again: "the
fashion of this world is passing off the stage" (1 Cor 7:31). In
this sense it is profoundly true that "the Lord is near" (Phil
4:5), his reentry into our world is a contemporary reality, thus
providing the Christian with that supernatural reassurance, that
inner sense of security, *(to epieikes)* which must, by the living
out of the Christian life *as a radiantly human life,* "become
known to all men."

What specific help did the apostolic Church offer the believer in order to aid him in the necessary business of participating in the paschal mystery by which he alone is to be redeemed? She provided the Christian with two essential means of assistance: the sacraments and "the Word of this salvation" (Acts 13:26), the gospel. Since we are not concerned at the moment with the first of these, suffice it to say here that the sacraments are simply a series of most basic human experiences, now elevated to the status of grace-bearing events, by the fact that Christ, to redeem man, has himself passed through and so transfigured the most significant activities of human life (being born, eating, suffering, dying). The contemplation of the Scriptures, however, also possesses an inalienable character as saving event—the object of our present investigation.

The gospel, the fundamental message of the Christian Church, assumed already in apostolic times three important forms. It was, in the first place, proclaimed to "those outside" the Christian community in order to produce *metanoia,* that radical religious reorientation of man which is conversion to the Christian faith. As such it is denominated in the New Testament as *kerygma,* the "heralding" of redemption in Jesus Christ (1 Cor 1:21), or *euangelion,* the "good news" of salvation (1 Cor 4:15). It was created by "the Twelve" (who had evolved into the apostolic college in the Christian Church) out of the teaching of Jesus and their own personal experience of the most significant events of Jesus' public ministry, passion, death and resurrection (Acts 1:21). Thus the apostles fulfilled their office as "witnesses of his resurrection" (Acts 1:22) to those who had not yet received the gift of Christian faith.

The second stage in the formulation of the gospel is represented by "the *didachē* (teaching) of the apostles" (Acts 2:42), delivered *within* the Christian community, in order to provide those who already accepted Christ with a deeper insight into the meaning of the paschal mystery (Acts 4:33). This message, communicated "from faith to faith" (Rom 1.17), by believers to believers, consisted essentially (as has already been noted) of the good news that "Jesus is Lord!" For it is precisely her keen awareness of this lordship of the exalted Christ which best

distinguishes the Church from "the world," which by definition
is ignorant of the truth that "Jesus is Lord!" This same sensitivity of Christian faith to the dynamic, saving truth that the
glorified Jesus is Master of history provided the apostolic church
with her missionary elan, driving her "to go and make disciples
of all the nations" (Mt. 28:19).

It is of course the third and final form of the Christian
gospel which constitutes the special object of our present concern: the articulation and formulation of the apostolic *diduchē*
in the four written gospels and in the other books of the New
Testament. With the genesis of this sacred body of Christian-
inspired literature we shall presently deal. For the moment we
wish to draw attention to one characteristic of the canonical
gospels, which may well appear to contradict what was asserted
earlier regarding the lack of nostalgia on the part of the apostolic
college for the earthly life of Jesus, "the days of his flesh" (Heb
5:7). It is surely obvious to anyone, who has even a nodding
acquaintance with the gospels, that by far the greater portion
of these narratives is devoted to accounts of the public ministry
of Jesus, "beginning from Galilee ... in the country of the Jews
and in Jerusalem ..." (Acts 10:37-39).

Why then, if it be true (as it assuredly is) that the apostles
had no desire to return to that apparently idyllic existence
during the years when they had followed Jesus personally, witnessed his miracles, heard his teaching, do our evangelists devote
almost all their written works to the recording of "what Jesus
began to do and to teach" (Acts 1:1)? The answer lies undoubtedly in their conviction that it was precisely through the prayerful assimilation of Jesus' earthly history that the Christian must
be led to a personal participation in the paschal mystery. Mark
states the principle thus (and he is echoed faithfully by the
three other evangelists): "If a man decides to come after me,
he must say 'no' to himself, shoulder his cross and follow me"
(Mk 8:34). To be a genuine disciple of Jesus, the Christian
must repeat in his own life—and expressly at the cost of his own
ego, as Mark immediately adds in the passage just cited—the
redeeming experiences of Jesus' own mortal existence.

Since a correct and profound comprehension of the implications of this crucial principle is basic to the living of the
Christian life in every age and culture, we must now reflect
upon its meaning at some length. For there is a third dimension
of meaning discoverable in the credal formula, "Jesus is Lord!",
and it explains the conundrum adverted to above, namely, the
seemingly disportionate space and attention devoted to the
public ministry of Jesus by men like the evangelists, who at the
same time did not regard this period as a vanished "golden age"
to which they longed to return.

The author of the Apocalypse hints at the solution of this
problem, when he presents the exalted Lord Jesus as Master of
history by means of the symbol of a lamb "standing as though
slain" (Ap 5:6). It is one of the most moving moments in the
entire book, a dramatic presentation, in the apocalyptic key, of
the gospel. The seer is granted a vision of heaven, which he
represents to his reader as the throne room of an ancient Near
Eastern court (Ap 4:1; 5:14). God the Father, as divine monarch
of the entire universe, is seated upon a throne, holding in his
right hand a scroll sealed with seven seals. Not improbably, the
scroll is intended to symbolize the Old Testament "Scriptures,"
which our author believes to contain the key to the interpretation
of the future history of this world. There is some consternation
amongst the heavenly senate, when no one can be found "worthy
to open the scroll by breaking its seals" (Ap 5:2). The Christian
prophet himself bursts into tears of grief, "because no one was
found worthy to open the scroll or to read it" (Ap 5:4), until
he is reassured by one of the heavenly retinue of elders. The unexpected appearance of the exalted Christ is greeted with a
joyous "new song" by the court of heaven (Ap 5:9 ff.).

It is thus, by means of such brilliant imagery, that our
author seeks to impress his reader with the all-important truth
that the exalted Christ has not merely chosen to remain man
throughout eternity, but has also elected to wear in glory the
badges of his sacred passion. Stated in somewhat more prosaic
fashion, the message of this grandiose vision is that Jesus Christ,
become Master of history through his earthly life, death and

resurrection, *is what he now is* in virtue of his past existence upon earth. That is to say, the modality of the lordship of the risen Christ has been determined by the mysteries of his earthly history. A consequence of this, as will be seen presently, is that these mysteries provide the Christian with a means of approach to the Lord Jesus. Or, conversely, it is through these mysteries that Christ now exerts, through the operation of his Spirit, his influence upon the life of the Christian. If he depicts the Lord Jesus as eternally adorned with the stigmata of his sacred passion, the seer has thereby called our attention to this significant theological truth by selecting the one most striking event in Jesus' mortal life: his passion and death. What our author clearly implies however is that *all the mysteries of Jesus' earthly history,* from the cradle to the grave, have been mysteriously endowed in his glorified humanity with a totally new and enduring *actuality.* The saving mysteries of the incarnation, birth, childhood and public life of Jesus Christ, with his temptations, triumphs, frustrations, disillusionment, retain in him, as he now exists, a perennial, dynamic reality, which remains ever contemporary with the ongoing process of history. The seer of Patmos had already suggested this same truth in the inaugural vision with which his book opens, where he represented the risen Christ as declaring, "I was dead, but remember, I am alive for evermore!" (Ap 1:18). Here we discover the Christian answer to the question of modern man, "Why contemplate the earthly history of Jesus?", alluded to earlier in this paper.

The passages from the Apocalypse exemplify the profound differences that distinguish the contemplation of the earthly life of Jesus Christ from any consideration of the life of Socrates. The most palpable and decisive difference of course springs from the fact that Jesus is the incarnate Son of God, whose earthly life was primarily a mission from the Father, in order to reveal that God whom "no man has ever seen" (Jn 1:18), through these very mysteries of his earthly career. But Socrates is dead, and the example of his life, however noble, is in large measure a matter of past history. However, it will not weaken but rather assist our argument if we recall that Socrates still survives in some very true sense, and his past survives in that survival. Do we not owe to Socrates' celebrated pupil and principal biographer the classical argument for the immortality of the soul?

Two points may serve to underscore the difference of which we speak. First, it is the conviction of the authors of the New Testament that the general resurrection (inaugurated indeed by Jesus' own resurrection) has not yet taken place, but awaits the consummation of this world's history. Accordingly, Socrates' past (the set of human experiences which constituted it) has not gone forward into that new life with God, as has the sacred humanity of Jesus Christ. In the second place, the writings of Plato are not inspired: they lack that unique quality which makes our gospels a privileged locus of the special presence of the Spirit of the risen Christ. Consequently, Socrates' past survives in a manner very different from that of the exalted Lord Jesus. The example of his life is transmitted to us by means of the literary genius of Plato, not through the Spirit-filled testimony of the evangelists, whose witness of apostolic faith is the foundation of the belief of the twentieth-century Christian. They attest the truth that Jesus Christ is "alive forevermore!" That is to say, Jesus has not simply returned to this life. He has gone forward to a totally new life with God his Father—and this in the entirety of his human nature with the whole gamut of his historical experiences. Thus all the mysteries of his life upon earth have been given a new reality in him who has become Master of history.

This truth of our Christian faith has enormous consequences for that kind of Christian prayer, which constitutes the warp and woof of the *Spiritual Exercises,* created by St. Ignatius: the *contemplatio.* It reminds us that the contemplation of the Gospel scenes is no mere exercise in imagination, no mere effort at reconstruction or recall (as with the modern historian) of events whose reality lies solely in the past. The events of Jesus' life, his words and teaching, are endowed perpetually with a contemporaneity or actuality in the risen Christ, such as the experiences of no other human being (with the exception of our Lady) are known to possess. The point is of such paramount importance that it may be useful to restate it in another way.

The problem, continually confronting the Christian in any age (as has already been said) is one of relating himself in most personal fashion to the risen Lord Jesus. At first sight the difficulty involved in such an enterprise may well appear insuperable. How can I, in my present existence, involved as I am in the universal human predicament of selfishness, of captivation by evil, of insecurity, and of resistance to the evolutionary process of my own transfiguration in the paschal mystery (all of them the effects of original sin), ever hope to relate myself to Christ who is so far above and beyond my reach? How can I make more real and personal my commitment of faith to him who now appears as "the last Adam," the fullness of human perfection?

We may illustrate the serious nature of the problem by a modern parable. Suppose a young woman falls in love with an atomic physicist, although she has neither the talent, interest nor possibility of relating to him on his own level of scientific achievement, which enables him to relate easily to his own colleagues. It is surely obvious that the only way such a woman can relate to such a man, and so lead a successful married life with him, is on some level other than that of atomic physics. In short, she must relate to him in *love* not on his level, but *on her own*.

The relationship of the Christian to the exalted Christ is somewhat analogous. I can only relate in faith to Jesus Christ on that level of the spiritual life *at which I now find myself*. Hence the profound significance of the contemplation of the mysteries of Jesus' earthly history. It is through these human experiences, which befell the Word incarnate "in the days of his flesh," that I am offered the possibility of relating myself to him who is my Savior. Happily, as my Christian faith tells me, these mysteries do not merely belong to the past as past, they are in fact an integral part of his present, glorified existence; and so are contemporary in a very real sense with my own life.

A proper understanding of the implications of this aspect

of the present status of the risen Christ provides an answer to a question that has been sometimes agitated in recent years. The question may be thus formulated: "Can I pray to Jesus *now*, as he *was* during his mortal life?" To be specific, is it possible to pray to the infant Jesus, the Jesus of the temptations, when I am fully aware that Christ now exists only as the exalted Lord?

In the light of the principle we have been discussing, I believe it is possible to answer this question, once it is properly formulated. The exalted Christ is what he now is precisely in virtue of these mysteries. By that statement is meant that Christ would not be the Lord of history in the way in which he actually is, were it not for the experiences of his earthly life. To say this, moreover, is to say more than is implied in the familiar proverb, "the boy is father to the man." There is a sense in which any of us are what we are in large measure as a result of our own past. Jesus Christ risen with his sacred humanity provides the ground of existence for these mysteries in a far more real and dynamic manner. The seer of Patmos asserts this by presenting him as "a lamb standing as though slain" (Ap 5:6). The author of Hebrews underscores the same truth by his declaration of faith in "Jesus Christ *yesterday and today the same*—and so forever" (Heb 13:8).

For example, I can then relate to the exalted Lord in his experience of temptation, because that experience retains its actuality in him as he now exists. Indeed, since I can only relate to him on that spiritual level at which I now find myself, whether in temptation, in suffering, in apostolic activity, etc., it is to these mysteries that my prayer to be effective is of necessity to be oriented. For if I am ultimately to be redeemed by accepting my own death, in all its concrete circumstances, from the hand of the Father (as Jesus himself did in order to effect the redemption of mankind), I must throughout my life be assimilated gradually more and more to Jesus Christ, in whom the paschal mystery is now completely realized. This means that the Christian life is a graduated process in which, over and over again, I am "elected" by God in Christ with my own free cooperation. The election constitutes, in my opinion, an essential part of the

Spiritual Exercises. This becomes clear once it is understood
that it possessed for St. Ignatius a profoundly biblical sense (cf.
Is 43:1-7), *i.e.,* it is primarily God's election of myself in Christ.
Thus it is not merely an ethical act of man's free will, depending
largely upon effective psychology: it depends fundamentally
upon the divine goodness and initiative, to which I am led to
respond with "the obedience of faith" (Rom 1:5).

It is this basic truth which St. Ignatius understood so deeply,
a truth which governed, more than mere logic or psychology,
the structuring of the *Spiritual Exercises.* This little book is most
basically a precious recipe for advancing step by step in the
"imitation of Christ," *i.e.,* the gradual realization in a most
personal manner of the grace of Christian baptism. As I grow
spiritually, I must constantly relate myself to Christ in the
various mysteries of his human history, through which he himself advanced to be "constituted Son of God in power by resurrection from death, in accordance with the Spirit of holiness"
(Rom 1:4). The sacraments are the most effective aid the Christian possesses in this participation in the paschal mystery, as
Paul so clearly saw. "Those of us who have been baptized into
Christ Jesus (the risen Christ) have been baptized into his
death" (Rom 6:3). Baptism is the sacramental experience of
Jesus' "death," if by that term we understand the whole gamut
of our Lord's personal experience of human mortality, all the
mysteries of his earthly history. For Paul the work of our redemption was accomplished through Jesus' death and resurrection.
Elsewhere in the New Testament (notably in the fourth Gospel),
the incarnation and the mysteries of Jesus' earthly life are considered part of this saving process. It is baptism, then, that
"authenticates" that series of basic human experiences through
which I am gradually transfigured in the image of my Lord.

But while baptism and all the sacraments are truly effective
in a way that transcends all personal human effort (*ex opere
operato,* as theologians assert), still my transformation in the
paschal mystery, because it is the very personal work of my own
redemption, must become for me a profoundly personal experience. It can never be conceived as an automatic process, whereby

I am redeemed unwittingly or unwillingly. If it be true that I am to be redeemed by Christ, it is also true that I am, in the very process of my own redemption, to act as a "redeemer." It is for this reason above all that I must relate to the Lord Jesus in the mysteries of his earthly history. Among the various ways in which I may accomplish this, *the* manner *par excellence* for the Christian, as St. Ignatius was so well aware, remains the contemplation (or meditation) of that earthly history *presented to me in the gospels.* I must develop some awareness of this presentation by the evangelists (and not content myself with imagining how the event might have occurred). By attending to the very personal way in which each sacred writer has narrated the event, I begin to grasp his individual approach to Christ, his "spirituality."

This means surely that the contemplation of God's Word in Scripture must truly be for me a saving event *(Heilsgeschehen).* The event-quality of this supremely significant spiritual exercise must be properly understood and appreciated, if it is to be efficacious in my Christian life. Accordingly, it is to a discussion of the event-character of this Christian contemplation that we wish to devote the second part of this little study. How can the Ignatian *contemplatio* result in a *Heilsgeschehen?* What approach to the gospels must be adopted, in order to effect such a saving experience with the grace of Christ? Before we discuss the technique which through faith leads to my participation in such a saving event, we must recall the manner in which our inspired authors (and we shall confine ourselves mainly to the evangelists) came to compose the gospels.

II. CREATION OF THE GOSPELS AND OF THE NEW TESTAMENT

We may begin with a general description of the process which led to the creation of our sacred literature in the Old Testament as well as in the New Testament. This will be seen upon analysis to consist of three principal moments: (1) *experience* of God's working from within history (and this involves the *reaction of faith* on the part of the individual or the collectivity, vouchsafed upon a privileged revelation); (2) a period of *theological reflection,* animated by faith, upon the data thus revealed, and (3) the *formulation of the experience* with its concomitant reflection, in an attempt to communicate this revelation in writing to the present and particularly future generations of believers.

Since the religion of Israel and especially Christianity itself make the claim to be historical religions, the faith of both necessarily took its rise from *an event,* the sign or medium of God's self-revelation *from within the historical process.* This primordial event was experienced by a nucleus of the future People of God: a group of runaway Hebrew slaves fleeing from their Egyptian taskmasters in the first instance, and in the second, "the Eleven," the first disciples, "with the women and Mary, the mother of Jesus, and his brothers" (Acts 1:14). The event which created Israel as God's "acquisition" was the exodus (by which term is to be understood the escape from Egypt through the Red Sea, the Sinai covenant, the wandering in the desert, the entry into the promised land). The event in the history of the Church corresponding to the exodus is Pentecost (which here signifies the entire paschal mystery at the climax of the earthly history of Jesus, his passion, exaltation and sending of the Spirit). No collectivity of human beings becomes a people without a sense of its destiny, an awareness of the direction of its history. Israel acquired this self-consciousness by the exodus; the Church was given it through the Lord Jesus' gift of his Spirit.

An integral part of this basic experience of God's action in history is, of course, the gift of faith which becomes the criterion *par excellence* for interpreting the experience and accepting the divine revelation communicated by God's loving, free choice of this people. In the light of this divinely given insight into their own historical experiences, not only was the significance of the past clarified, but each successive crisis in the life of the people could be confronted, comprehended and surmounted. For Yahweh's purpose relative to Israel was continually manifested through the centuries, until during the Babylonian exile its prophets and priests (filled with the dynamic hope of a final intervention of their God in their history) were able to undertake the collection, codification and interpretation of Israel's traditions, ritual and laws. It was then that the Old Testament, as we know it, began to be written—the resultant of Israel's experience of God's action in its national history and its conviction that, through tragedy and triumph, "God had visited his people." What gives Israel's national literature its unique character is the fact that it is a national history written not to glorify the nation, but the nation's God. And the fact that this national literature was written at all is proof of the authors' conviction that their insight into the divine meaning of this history contained a God-given message intended for future generations of their own people, indeed possibly of the whole of mankind. At the origin of these writers' labors lay the firm belief, however vaguely grasped, that their work was inspired by the God who had graciously disclosed to them his mysterious operations in history.

To say that Pentecost is the decisive happening which led to the recording of Christian sacred history in the New Testament may well seem surprising, since the coming of the Holy Spirit had been preceded by the apostles' experience of the earthly life of Jesus during his public ministry, passion and glorification. Yet it was Pentecost that dispelled the ambiguity and mystery which had enshrouded the precious experiences of the Twelve during Jesus' earthly existence. They had indeed witnessed his miracles, followed him with love and loyalty, preserved their fellowship even after his departure from them. Yet throughout this entire privileged period they did not know who he actually was: the Son of God incarnate. "After Jesus had risen from the dead, and when his divinity was clearly perceived, the faith of the disciples, far from blotting out the remembrance of the events that had happened, rather consolidated it, since their faith was based on what Jesus had done and taught."[12] The pentecostal revelation brought these disciples of Jesus the realization, through Christian faith, of their own new identity as the new Israel. It marked also the inauguration of the apostolic practice of the Christian sacraments. It gave rise to the creation of the *kerygma*, the gospel, by the apostolic college.

Yet this primitive proclamation, to judge by the authentic samples or résumés of the apostolic preaching preserved in Acts, was far from complete. It omitted certain important doctrinal affirmations, e.g., the Incarnation, preexistence of Christ, his priestly character, the sacrificial significance of his death and resurrection. Deeper theological reflection was required, as well as further effort at articulating the Christian message. Hence it is no accident that the first contribution to the New Testament was made by Paul in the form of a series of letters in which this great religious genius struggled, with the aid of "the Scriptures" and his acquaintance with Hellenistic culture, to give theological expression to his profound insight into the Christian mystery. It was only after and as a result of Paul's contribution, particularly to the Christian understanding of the paschal mystery, that our gospels could be written. For the gospels, despite their apparent artlessness, are unquestionably the supreme literary and christological achievement of the apostolic age. *"The sacred authors,* for the benefit of the churches, took this earliest body of instruction, which had been handed on orally at first and then in writing . . . and set it down in the four gospels. In doing this each of them followed a method suitable to the special purpose which he had in view. Out of the material which they had received, the sacred authors selected especially those items which were adapted to the varied circumstances of the faithful as well as to the end which they themselves wished to attain; these they recounted in a manner consonant with those circumstances and with that end. The results of recent study have made it clear that the teachings and the life of Jesus were not simply recounted for the mere purpose of being kept in remembrance, but were 'preached' in such a way as to furnish the Church with the foundation on which to build up. faith and morals."[13]

The preceding, somewhat hasty description of the three main stages through which the Bible came into existence can now serve to illustrate the sense in which the modern Christian contemplation of the mysteries of Jesus' earthly life can, in fact *ought,* to be effectively carried out. This contemplation or meditation must terminate *in an event,* a saving event, which is meant to happen to the Christian in prayer. For only thus can he be transfigured progressively by the paschal mystery already incarnate in the risen Christ. Indeed only by the personal assimilation of these mysteries from the mortal life of Jesus Christ can the believer relate (at his own present level of Christian existence) to his redeemer. If his redemption is to become, as it necessarily must, his own most personal achievement in Christ, the efficacious action of the sacraments in his life must be accompanied by his wholehearted, conscious and deliberate self-commitment to him who is Lord of history (and hence Master of the individual Christian's life). This is the basic reason for the extraordinarily striking assertion of the Vatican II in *Dei Verbum:* "The Church has always venerated the divine Scriptures just as she venerates the body of the Lord, since from the table of both the word of God and of the body of Christ she unceasingly receives and offers to the faithful the bread of life, especially in the sacred liturgy.... Therefore, like the Christian religion itself, all the preaching of the Church must be nourished and ruled by sacred scripture."[14]

How should the Ignatian *contemplatio* of the mysteries of our Lord's earthly life be carried out? Given the stated purpose of this spiritual exercise—to acquire "an interior knowledge of our Lord, who for me is made man, that I may the more love him and follow him" (104)—it becomes evident that the method to be employed is actually *the reverse of the process* through which our gospels came into existence. For that knowledge which St. Ignatius describes as "interior" is a truly experiential knowledge absorbing the Christian totally in the innermost part of his being. It is not merely intellectual, "notional knowledge" in Cardinal Newman's phrase, but "real knowledge," possessing an essential event-quality.

Accordingly, the believer must begin with the sacred text of the gospel narrative, since it is by its inspired character the *locus privilegiatus* of the action of the Spirit of the exalted Lord Jesus. If he is now present in this world, as the Christian faith asserts, by a dynamic involvement in the contemporary historical process, he is present in a unique way in the gospels, just as he is uniquely present in the eucharist. As Father Roderick Mac-Kenzie, S.J., rector of the Pontifical Biblical Institute, has observed, "in this respect (as in others) an illuminating comparison can be drawn between the scriptures and the eucharist ... the eucharist is not something that the Church herself instituted; it too is a gift from her Spouse, a divine creation. ... It too is *a means and manifestation of Christ's presence among his members.* Thus both scripture and eucharist are part of the Church's divinely bestowed equipment for carrying on *the Savior's work of redemption.*"[15]

In order to collaborate in the saving event which is the intended goal of the Ignatian *contemplatio,* the Christian of the twentieth century must begin with the sacred text itself, the inspired expression of the religious experience of the evangelist, the result of his personal confrontation (and that of the apostolic Church, whose special witness he is) with the exalted Lord Jesus. To realize effectively here and now a similar confrontation the modern believer must labor to grasp the significance of the words in which the gospel scene is couched, appreciating the literary form of the narrative, penetrating the figures of speech, the peculiarities if idiom, perceiving (above all) the particular purpose or christological import of the passage. To the best of his abilities he must make his own the conviction of Pius XII, that "it is absolutely necessary for the interpreter to go back in spirit to those remote centuries of the East."[16] For such an enterprise, far from leading to mere sciolism, is a necessary preparation for the personal encounter with the glorified Christ.

Here it may be helpful to recall the valuable lesson which the practitioners of the method of Gospel study know as *Formgeschichte* have taught us: that the words and deeds of Jesus were formulated by our evangelists not with a view to producing an impersonal, colorless, "objective" account, but to provide something much more valuable. Moreover, the authority of these sacred authors reposes *primarily,* not upon the accuracy or fidelity of the memories of "the original eyewitnesses" (Lk

1:2), but rather upon their Spirit-filled insight into the meaning of the sayings and doings of Jesus. The gospels do not simply give cold facts about our Lord; they record his words and actions as understood, selected, interpreted and *lived* by these privileged witnesses to the faith of the apostolic Church. It is highly important to remember that the "life setting" *(Sitz im Leben)* of the gospel accounts was the daily life of the first and second generations of Christians, and not the historical context in which the events originally occurred. Thus these sacred narratives put us in touch with the living faith of the Church in the first century of her existence, and with her daily life lived by the gospel.

A proper appreciation of this saving character of the truth exhibited by the gospels will provide invaluable aid in the second step toward the *Heilsgeschehen* which is the goal of the *contemplatio,* that is, the modern Christian's personal theological reflection upon the text. The revelation of the mysteries of Jesus' earthly life which the text contains is communicated together with the precious religious experience by the apostolic Church of these very mysteries. Because the sacred text conveys this revelation about Jesus of Nazareth incarnated in the reaction of faith of its sacred author (and of the Christian community that stands behind him), it is capable of producing a similar reaction of faith in the twentieth-century believer.

How does one conduct theological reflection upon a narrative in the gospels? The technique may be reduced to one simple, searching question: What is the Lord Jesus attempting to say *to me now* through this particular text of the gospel? If I can plumb the depths of meaning in the words of the evangelist to the best of my ability and with the power of my faith, I shall assimilate them to myself, or better, I shall be disposed *to be assimilated* or conformed to the mystery which I am contemplating.

The final step in the exercise of contemplation is the religious experience, the "saving event." One might best describe it by saying that the mystery must happen for me, to me. The process is described in a very ancient Christian text in speaking of our Lord's nativity. "He it is who is from the beginning, who appears as new and is discovered to be ancient, yet continually born anew in the hearts of the saints" (*Epistle to Diognetus*, XI, 4) . The same idea is found in the text of the *Spiritual Exercises:* the colloquy of the contemplation on the Incarnation speaks of "our Lord thus newly incarnate" (109), while that on the nativity directs the exercitant "to see . . . the child Jesus from the time he is born" (114) ; "in order that after such toils . . . he may die on the cross, and all this for me . . ." (116). It is thus in the Old Testament that the sixth-century author of Deuteronomy described the event-character of the ritual proclamation of Yahweh's covenant to his own contemporaries, many centuries after Israel's great initial experience at Sinai. It is instructive to note how the author phrases this covenant renewal. "Yahweh our God made a covenant *with us* at Horeb. It was not with our ancestors that Yahweh made this covenant, but *with ourselves who are all here alive today"* (Dt. 5:2-3) . Similarly, when I reflect upon the parable of the Good Samaritan (Lk 10:30 ff.) , I must consider Jesus' final words as addressed to myself in my contemporary situation: "Go, and do likewise yourself!"

The creator of this saving event, in which my contemplation is designed to terminate, is the Spirit of the risen Christ, who through his intimate presence in the believer makes the mystery happen for him. St. Paul has described this Christian religious experience in two striking passages, where he speaks, not of any mystical phenomenon, but of the prayer life of every sincere Christian. The first text occurs in Romans 8:15-16: "Those who are led by the Spirit of God are God's sons. For you have not received the mentality of slavery (forcing you back) again into fear: you have received the mentality proper to your adoption as sons, thanks to which we cry '*Abba*' (dear Father!) ." The other Pauline passage (Gal 4:6) is frequently mistranslated, with the result that its meaning is lost. "The proof that you are sons is that God has sent the Spirit of his Son into our hearts crying, '*Abba*' (dear Father!) ." Thus for St. Paul the *Heilsgeschehen* of which we are speaking is an experiential awareness of our relationship as sons and daughters to God as Father. Indeed for the apostle the whole orientation of the Christian existence is toward an ever profounder consciousness of this special relationship. St. Ignatius himself seems to have the same conception in mind when he stresses the necessity for the Jesuit of cultivating what he calls *familiaritas cum Deo in oratione*. The phrase is properly understood as the acquiring of a "sense of family," God's family, through prayer. And (as it would appear from the frequency with which St. Ignatius recommends the *contemplatio* in his *Spiritual Exercises*), it is chiefly by the contemplation of the earthly mysteries of Jesus' life that this "sense of family" can best be cultivated and made more actual to oneself.

How real and personal this Christian awareness of such divine adoptive sonship was to the mind of St. Paul may be gauged by recalling that the Aramaic term *Abba* was a term of such familiarity (it was used in Palestinian families of Jesus' day by children toward their fathers) that no Jew dared use this form of address in prayer to God. When, as he customarily did, the Jew prayed to God as Father, he said "Our Father, the One in heaven"—precisely the Matthean version of the Lord's prayer (Mt 6:9). It is highly significant that during Jesus' earthly life *only he* is represented in the gospels (Mk 14:36) as addressing God in this familiar way.

It remains to suggest some explanation of how our contemplation of the mysteries of Jesus' earthly history is truly efficacious in assisting us to advance in this consciousness of our relationship as sons to the heavenly Father. The answer quite simply is that it was through these very events that Jesus himself deepened his sense of his unique filial relationship to the Father. For it was through his experience of those events in his own earthly life that our Lord's human nature was gradually transformed by the paschal mystery, which reached its culmination in his death and resurrection. This statement may sound somewhat strange to us, until we recall Paul's startling assertion that Jesus Christ was "constituted Son of God in power by resurrection from death in accordance with his Spirit of holiness" (Rom 1:4). There is then a very real sense in which this sonship of the incarnate Son was only fully realized at the climax of his earthly career.

Now, as we stated earlier, the exalted Christ is *what he now is* in virtue of his past. These very mysteries of his earthly life effectively determine his status as Lord of history, and so retain in the contemporary Christ their actuality and contemporaneity. But this exaltation of the Lord Jesus as Master of history means, according to the faith of the primitive Church, his deeper involvement in the historical process. That is to say, the glorified Christ is dynamically present to me in the present age, effecting my transfiguration as a Christian in the paschal mystery, molding me in his own image (Rom 8:29). And moreover it is through these various mysteries of his earthly existence (perpetually real and actual in himself) that he can "touch" me in the innermost recesses of my being, imparting to me the grace-filled capability of relating to him in these very mysteries. For it is my Christian destiny, the real possibility of which was conferred by my baptism, to become, through my own death (accepted in filial obedience from the hand of the Father) and resurrection, a son of God in the unique Son of God (*filius in Filio*). It is ever to this eschatological sonship that the presence of the Spirit of God within me leads, as St. Paul well knew. "Not only that, but we ourselves who possess the first fruits of the Spirit articulate our yearning in the inmost depths of our being, as we await expectantly our adoptive sonship, the redemption of our bodies" (Rom 8:23). St. Luke repeats the theme by means of his version of Jesus' words to the Sadducees in the controversy over the general resurrection. "They cannot die any more, since they are like angels; and they are sons of God since they are sons of the resurrection" (Lk 20:36).

Notes

1 *Editor's Note:* Since being presented at the Shrub Oak Symposium this paper has appeared in *Theological Studies,* to which grateful acknowledgment is made for permission to republish it here.

2 In a letter to the International Congress on the Spiritual Exercises held at Loyola, Spain, in August 1966.

3 The numbers in parentheses are references to the text of the *Spiritual Exercises,* most readily available to English readers in Louis J. Puhl, S.J.,

The Spiritual Exercises of St. Ignatius: A New Translation (Westminster, Md., 1965) .

4 *Acta Apostolicae Sedis* 35 (1943) 310.

5 *Ibid.*, 311.

6 *The Documents of Vatican II,* ed. Walter M. Abbott, S.J. (New York, 1966) , p. 127.

7 *Ibid.*, p. 468.

8 Cf. *Dei Verbum*, No. 11, *op. supra laudato,* p. 119.

9 Cf. *Documents of the Thirty-first General Congregation,* ed. Donald R. Campion, S.J. (Woodstock, Md., 1967) , p. 42.

10 Cf. D. M. Stanley, *The Apostolic Church in the New Testament* (Westminster, Md., 1965) , pp. 104-106.

11 "Jesus' name," *i.e., Kyrios,* bestowed upon him by the Father at his glorification. As the allusion to Is 45:22-24 indicates, it is an expression of his divinity.

12 "Instructio de historical Evangeliorum veritate," in *Acta Apostolicae Sedis* 56 (1964) 714.

13 *Ibid.*, 715.

14 *The Documents of Vatican II,* p. 125.

15 R. A. F. MacKenzie, S.J., *Introduction to the New Testament,* 2d ed. (Collegeville, Minn., 1965) , p. 52.

16 *Acta Apostolicae Sedis* 35 (1943) 314-315.

simple prayer in a sophisticated world

ROBERT J. O'CONNELL, S.J.

I must begin by apologizing. I don't know quite how I wound up being here in the first place. Father Orsy keeps insisting I ought to be in theology rather than in philosophy, but that just proves, if further proof were needed, what a lovely fey sense of humor he has. Or maybe what a dreadful state contemporary theology is in. As an outsider, I had no notion things were quite so bad as that!

My feeling here is that of the outsider: like a jay among nightingales—or in today's parlance, a hawk among doves. For, in Pascal's celebrated phrase, what can the God of our Fathers, the God of Abraham and Isaac and Jacob—and of the Lord Jesus Christ—what can *that* God have to do with the God of the philosophers?

In Pascal's sense those two Gods don't have too much to do with each other: Pascal was right in intimating that no man can *pray to* the God of the "philosophers." To the God of the philosophers he was talking about, that is. But in another sense, those Gods have had entirely *too much* to do with each other. They have gotten mixed up with each other to the point where the God of the philosophers—the God of the sophisticated world view each one of us takes in with the very air we breathe—has very nearly eclipsed the God of that simple kind of prayer that Jesus of Nazareth practiced and enjoined upon his followers to practice.

Finally, I would like to direct your minds (and my own) toward taking another look at the God of the philosophers— but to a God the philosophers, some of them at least, and to my mind the best of them, don't talk too much about; a God who is really, at the best of their moments and when they are at the very top of their form, the God they worship, and to whom they can pray. I won't say too much about that God, because if he's really God after all, there's not too much we can say about him. It will be enough, and more than satisfy my modest ambitions, if I can direct your minds toward him, get them to feel the stretch involved in reaching out for what the Bible speaks of as a glimpse of his face or, more to my purpose here, the touch of his hand.

I.   JESUS' WORLD VIEW

Let me begin by quoting somewhat extensively from a book that I think still stands as a great book, Karl Adam's *Son of God*.[1] It comes as something of a shock to realize that even the English translation dates from nearly forty years ago. Adam sketches Jesus' interior life: the kind of prayer-relation he constantly entertained with his Father. He then goes on to describe the "objective religious reality," the "picture of God" and "view of the world" supposed by Jesus' "subjective act of prayer."

In the foreground of religious reality Jesus sees the all-operative, creative God. It is not to the far-off, wholly transcendental, silent God of contemporary Hellenism that he prays, nor is it to the God of mysticism, of the remote abode of the blessed, to which only the ecstatic soul may ascend. His God is the all-creative, all-operative God of Moses and the prophets—"My Father worketh until now, and I work" (Jn 5:17). His God clothes the lilies and feeds the ravens. And as he works in the life of nature so does he in that of history. All the leading spirits of humanity, the prophets and the Baptist, were sent by him. As the sheep to its shepherd so does man belong to his God (Lk 15:6). All upheavals and wars, every world event large and small is God's act. The entire history of mankind is for Jesus a revelation of the living God. And since he finds the creative will of his Father in all things and in all persons, he sees these things and these persons not from without in all the deceptiveness of their appearance, but from within in their essential relation to the will of God, as a revelation of his creative might, as the embodied will of his Father.

Adam goes on to show that Jesus' view of things catches them at the point
where: they proceed from the hand of the Creator. He sees them in their inner God-related dynamic, in the living flux of creation, in the creative process of their beginning in God. Hence these things are fundamentally at every moment subject to the divine call. They cannot take refuge from God behind the armor plates of any kind of order

of nature. Naked and bare they lie in the hand of the creating God, and they have no other surety of existence but that of his mighty will.

In Jesus' way of seeing, then, there lies "behind and beyond all things" not some

dead, soulless piece of mechanism, not any kind of Fate blindly working by natural laws, but absolute life and spirit, absolute mobility and spontaneity, in other words the freedom of God. Jesus lives on this freedom. To him God is absolute free will; absolute power, before which every other will and power are dust. Whoever has faith in this absolute power "and staggers not . . . shall say to this mountain. Take up and cast thyself into the sea, and it shall be done" (cf. Mt 21:21f; Lk 17:5f; 17:19; Mk 11:22f). Jesus can believe his Father capable of such incredible things because he sees everywhere and always the operative God at work. To him God is the immediate tangible reality, the being he meets first in all persons and things, the secret and profoundest meaning of all being, the reality of all realities. He apprehends the creative work of God directly in the here and now of things. For him it is no longer a belief but a direct vision . . . natural and obvious . . . [a] visual experience [that grounds] the reliance and confidence with which the human consciousness and will of Jesus transcend the possibilities open to created beings, in order to realize the possibilities of God, to work signs and wonders innumerable, not only the casting out of devils and the healing of the sick, but even the raising from the dead. "Father, I give thee thanks that thou hast heard me. And I know that thou hearest me always" (Jn 11:41f).

Now I must take it that you agree, at least in substance, that this *was* the world view Jesus lived by: the scriptural allusions with which Adam laces his text make that agreement relatively easy to furnish, I think. There is something disarmingly childlike about that view of the universe; something fresh, direct, immediate and liberating.

The world view of simple prayer

That world view grounded not only Jesus' own unhesitating

assumption that he could, through direct contact with the all-creative God, "transcend the possibilities open to created beings . . . to work signs and wonders innumerable"; it grounds not only his own "faith that will remove mountains," his own "trust which storms the heavens"; it grounds, as well, his repeated insistence that we too, his followers, share that faith, enjoy that trust and pray with the conviction that the Father hears us always, hears us and really answers us.

For if you look at the texts in the New Testament where Jesus urges us to pray, the prayer is simple; the simple-minded man's prayer, if you will, the prayer of petition: "Ask and you shall receive, knock and it will be opened to you." If we have faith, we too will move mountains; we must ask the Father anything—and everything—in his name, assured that if we who are evil know how to give our children good things when they ask for them, Our Father will respond to our asking by giving us, not a stone, but our "daily bread." And that kind of prayer, I suggest, supposes on our part much the same view of the universe as Adam portrays as Jesus' own. We are, in Adam's terms, called upon to pray not to some "far-off, wholly transcendental, silent God of . . . Hellenism, nor . . . to the God of mysticism . . . to which only the ecstatic soul may ascend," but to the God who clothes the lilies and feeds the ravens, to the God we can behold as operative in the simplest, most familiar of human and earthly realities, so that our heart leaps up with the spontaneous cry, "hallowed be thy name."

But is it possible, in the sophisticated world our science and philosophy now present to us for our assent, to pray that simple kind of prayer?

II. THE WORLD VIEW OF "CONTEMPORARY MAN"

For our world *has* become sophisticated: and that sophisticated world is one that the Christian believer takes in at every pore, assimilates with every book he reads, every ad he sees, every aspirin he swallows. Adam sketches it briefly, but tellingly, when depicting the world view that was *not* Jesus': one in which there tends to lie, behind and beyond all things, some "dead, soulless piece of mechanism . . . [some] kind of Fate blindly working by natural laws."

When Jesus speaks of the God who works, these words have a deeper and richer sound than in the mouth of ordinary pious folk, especially in these days when rationalism has stunted or destroyed the immediacy of religious experience in them. Jesus does not, like them, contemplate intermediate causes through which the creative God calls all becoming and being into existence. Still less do these intermediate causes combine for him into a constant self-sufficient order of nature looming up between Creator and creature as a rival cosmos of created causal sequences. Such a belief in a rigid order of nature Jesus never shared. Indeed, it would have seemed to him an idolatry of purely human conceptions and systems. For in the last resort it is man himself who has contrived and gone on contriving such laws and systems, in the hope by their help to master for the moment the colossal, unfathomable, inexhaustible mystery of reality and to repose therein for a little space. Jesus does not need such artificial aids to arrive at things. His approach to them is by way of God not of man. Jesus sees things not where they have already been rigidified for human thought into a fixed significance and being, but where they proceed from the hand of the Creator.

Nearly forty years ago, Karl Adam was addressing himself to the central problem that gave rise more recently to that curiously intense, but just as curiously short-lived phenomenon, the Death of God theologies. The question then was fundamentally the same as its more recent versions: Can the intelligent, well-read, acculturated twentieth-century man still accept as his own the world view that sustained Jesus in his prayer, the world view that grounded his injunction that we, too, should trustfully approach God, call him Father and cast our every care upon him?

The recent Death of God theologians gave basically divergent answers to their question. Adam's very terms remind one of Gabriel Vahanian's rejection of all human thought-systems as so many species of idolatry: the believer must profoundly suspect, even at the limit reject, the scientifico-philosophic constructs that fill the air and furnish the cultural atmosphere of our time. There can be, in Tertullian's ancient cry, no compact between Athens and Jerusalem: any effort to ally the perception of faith and the constructs of human intelligence will inevitably lead to the evacuation of faith itself. We must admit that the apparent Death of God really amounts to a profound sickness of modern man. We must shatter all our idols, and learn to wait without them.[2]

But there is, as you know, another, and opposite wing of Death-of-God-ism. And one feature about it is utterly fascinating. For the first time since the Reformation's radical rejection of fallen human nature and the perverse workings of fallen man's intelligence, a significant body of Protestant thought has taken human culture and intelligence with a seriousness that is, if anything, dreadfully unrelieved. A Hamilton, a Van Buren, and in some respects the early Cox,[3] would have us take the twentieth-century view of our universe so seriously, swallow it so uncritically, that there seems no room left for the God whom Jesus of Nazareth claimed was his Father. And no room left for praying to that God.

When twentieth-century man beholds his world, he inclines to see it as just that "constant, (if not 'rigid') self-sufficient order of Nature . . . a cosmos of created causal sequences." Adam (and Vahanian) stigmatize; a "soulless piece of mechanism" which advancing science has taken it as its province to explore, and advancing technology manipulates and more and more subdues to man's own purposes. In such a world, it makes no sense to call on God to relieve one's headache: we know the chemistry of headaches now, and television daily reminds us (however tastelessly, lugubriously) that there is aspirin, or better yet Excedrin, forever hovering over us to minister to our every need in that department. Instead of praying for our ailing infant, we make every effort to find the most competent medical skill that will promote the production of the antibodies needed to fight the infection. And for our spiritual needs, those deeper anxieties that tempt us still to think of man as needing more than science can furnish, there is always the tranquilizer, the dry martini, or the psychiatrist's couch.

For man, we are told, has "come of age"; he need no longer submit to nature's workings as though they were the moment-by-moment expression of some whimsical divinity, a divinity empowered to intervene at any point to turn off the spigots of suffering and flood our world instead with the waters of consolation. He must, instead, get cracking, bring to bear the resources and instruments our century puts at his command, and change in nature what he sees needs changing. More and more, he is become the master of his fate, the captain of his soul; both creature and controller of a world shorn of all meaningful relation to "another," higher world. God is a hypothesis for which he finds no longer any need. And prayer, especially the simple prayer of petition for our daily needs, has become not only an irrelevance: worse, it stands for a temptation; the temptation to retreat to that snuggling religiosity that characterized the infancy of our race.

What, then, is to be said about Jesus—about the kind of prayer he prayed and told us we must pray? The question becomes something of an embarassment, but (for this wing of the Death-of-God theologians) regularly takes the tack of shearing off that stratum of the gospel message that has to do with his relation to his Father, of treating it as mythology. We are then called upon to extract from the gospels the figure of a man who somehow—mysteriously and unaccountably (since it occurs without any relation to a loving Father he trusted through and beyond the jaws of death)—showed us how we can be "free." For Jesus was, assuredly, free of the fears and limits attendant on our ordinary humanity, superbly free to be a man "for others"; he was, beyond any doubt, the embodiment of an unreserved love for once uniquely realized by one of our poor confused race. But is this portrait of the human Christ, no longer Son of God—and Van Buren is honest enough to ask the question toward the end of his work—is this traditional Christianity in any recognizable sense? The touchstone of the answer, I suggest, is precisely this. In Van Buren's version of secular Christianity there is no room for the Our Father. Christianity has become an ethics; and Van Buren quite candidly admits that he, for one, no longer prays.

I've dwelt on these two strands of the Death of God theology because the movement is familiar and represents a challenge; and because some reputable theologians are known to have felt that the spirit evoked by these men was genuinely the spirit of our age, that the movement was a fairly accurate barometer of the weather prevailing in many a Christian heart as it suddenly found itself beating in a "post-Christian" epoch.

III.   AN ANCIENT PROBLEM

But I've deliberately introduced the issues raised by this movement by way of Karl Adam to bring to your attention that the problems our more recent theologians sometimes portray as bright new problems proper to our age—proper to a century when man had finally "come of age"—go back much much further in time. They go back, in fact, to the very roots of Western philosophical—and consequently theological—thinking.

Gilson, in his *God and Philosophy,* speaks of the ancient Greek mythologist's instinct for peopling the universe with personal divinities: an instinct that comes from deep within the human psyche. Unamuno gives that instinct a contemporary voice when he protests his aching reluctance to accept the verdict that man is "alone in the universe." Put in the somewhat more austere and antiseptic categories of causality, the argument runs this way: a universe that could give birth to the phenomenon of human personality must possess the hidden resources to account for that birth: it cannot itself, therefore, be totally impersonal. Whatever name one gives, accordingly, to the source or ground of all being, that name must designate a personal, or if you will a superpersonal, Being.

But the Greek transition from a mythological to a more scientific, or philosophical mode of thought, introduced another version of the universe. That version had by no means been absent from the mythological account of things, but now it came to the fore. The experience of order, of causal sequence, solicited the mind to view the workings of our world in more impersonal terms. It is difficult to recapture the pristine amazement that

came to the Pythagorean when he discovered that so many of the
phenomena in our experience betrayed the harmonies and relationships of the number series. No wonder, then, that the discovery was gradually extended to cover wider and wider circles
of experience—until all things became number and the soul
became the number of everything. The entire universe ran by
the numbers.

That strand of thought was not entirely absent from the
mythological view: indeed, the question had always run whether
the personal God whose name was Zeus was master of (or
himself subject to) the inexorable laws of the Destiny that
governed the course of all events. But with the advent of Greek
science, and with its corrosive critique of the fantasies and
capriciousness that so frequently characterized the mythological
mode of accounting for the universe, the way was prepared for
the triumph of the impersonal.

That triumph was bound to affect Western theology, particularly through those two great representatives of Greek
thought, Plato and Aristotle. It was facilitated somewhat by the
relatively undeveloped concept that Greek thought had of the
person; but its irony is nowhere more striking than in the development of Plato's thought.

For if there is one proposition that emerges from his master's
defense of his life before the Athenian court, it is this: Socrates
refuses to believe that what has happened to him has come about
mechanikôs—through the blind, inexorable working of an impersonal universe. No, for him, the crucial actors in the universe
of moral good and evil are the gods, and gods that are not un-
responsive to the good and evil men do. This, Socrates admits,
is his faith: *doxa, pistis,* but a sturdy faith, a solid hope.

It was, though, a faith facing challenges from all sides; a
hope too individual, too personal to sustain the ongoing moral
community that the Plato of the eventual *Republic* knew must
be sustained and preserved. How could one convert this faith
into knowledge, *epistêmê:* a knowledge that would both solidify
it and make it communicable to the insight of others? This, I
take it, was the great question Plato took it on himself to resolve.
And in the course of his development, there came to hand the

resources of the very mathematical mode of thought that tends, if anything, to dissolve the personal and guarantee the reign of impersonality, inexorability, determinism and necessity.

The twilight battle that is waged in Plato's writings between the personal gods of the old mythology and the grandiose, impersonal *Forms* he came to think as governing the phenomena of our sense world is too complicated to go into here. Suffice it to say that it is a battle, and one of which Plato was more than dimly aware—far more aware, I submit, than Leslie Dewart,[4] for one, seems to imagine. A battle that remains, on that account, more instructive than Dewart allows it to be.

That battle goes on, I suggest, in that great Christian Platonist, Augustine. Too little has been made of the fact that in the *Confessions* Augustine tells us as plainly as he could that his ideal of certainty, and consequently, his paradigm for conceiving what the perfection of truth and being might be, is the numerical equation: $7 + 3 = 10$. The *Contra Academicos* spells out this same viewpoint: the higher world, the "other world" not "of this world" that Christ claimed was his kingdom, is envisaged on the model of universal, necessary, analytic statements perfectly in keeping with the mathematical tradition of Platonism and Neo-Pythagoreanism. His master in thought, Plotinus, had roundly criticized the only version of Christianity he knew, Gnosticism, mostly because its scheme of salvation ran against his cherished idea of a perfectly ordered cosmos: a cosmos whose workings must, in the last analysis, respond to that strand of Hellenic thought that insisted on rational, quasi-mathematical intelligibility. How, then, can the Christian claim to contact (in Adam's terms), "behind and beyond all things . . . absolute life and spirit, absolute mobility and spontaneity, . . . the freedom of God"? The opening prayer of the *Soliloquies* shows Augustine already half-reflectively taking the measure of this issue: the God he prays to is the God of order, the God of inexorable law governing the revolutions of both stars and seasons and eons; and yet, he is at the same time the personal God, whom one can, in confessing, address as *Tu,* "thou." The world we experience is patterned on the world of the Divine Ideas; their shape in turn is determined largely by the mathematical approach Augustine

regularly takes to them: they are the fountainheads of that uni-
versality and necessity that prevails—the example comes back
again and again—in mathematical truths. And yet, that world of
ideas is fundamentally identical with the Eternal Christ; truth is
not merely some impersonal sea of being from which all subalt-
ern truths emanate; truth is Some-One, free and personal. And
still, when in the *De Trinitate* Augustine asks wherein the
character of soul as image of God resides, the answer comes: in
that part of the soul that makes it capable of grasping necessary,
immutable truths—and once again, the privileged examples are
mathematical. Should we, he asks significantly, figure our relation
to God on the model of a friend's relation to his friend? No:
better to think of our relation to God on the model of the eye's
relation to light. Augustine is thinking of the mind's relation to
that intelligible light whereby it is empowered to make the kinds
of judgment prized by the geometrician and the mathematician.
The possibility of envisaging our relation to God in frankly
interpersonal terms has been briefly entertained, but only to
be rejected.

How, then, can the Christian pray the Our Father? Saint
Thomas takes up the question in the *Secunda Secundae* (II, II,
83 a 2) . And, typically, his main concern is to save not the
dialogic relation of God as Some-One with the Christian as
some-one. He is bent, rather, on keeping intact the eternal
immutability of the divine plan for our world. The notion of
perfection as immutable and necessary dies hard.

And that, I submit, is the notion that still presides over
what the Death of God theologians deem to be contemporary
science's picture of the world: our world must be an ordered
world. Whitehead is eloquent on how touching modern science's
loyalty has been to that fundamental tenet of medieval theology.[5]
But what kind of order is in question? Again, Whitehead's
answer seems irrefutable: post-Renaissance science was, until
very recently, in its curious way, the child of Pythagoras: to
explain, to lay bare the order that governs the causal sequences
of our experience, eventually meant to measure, quantify and
mathematically relate the phenomena involved. The universe
runs by the numbers.

IV. THE CHOICE OF TODAY'S BELIEVER

How, then, is the believer to decide which of these versions of the universe he will accept? Is Jesus correct in seeing every-thing as radically and immediately related to the Father's creative freedom? as every moment coming toward us from this personal source? Or must the thinking, educated man of today accept the mathematically ordered world of science, its causal sequences governed by the inexorable and impersonal relation-ships of the number series? a world in which it is both useless and infantile to pray?

Which God are we to choose: the God of our Fathers—the God of the Our Father—or the God of the philosophers?

For in one sense every man must choose between these two worlds. Even if he be entirely innocent of the technical ins and outs of the question, the most rudimentarily cultivated man of today finds the totally secularized version of the universe seeping in on him at every pore, battering against his ears and flooding his visual space with its testimonials. The faith-enervating power of that world view is all the more enhanced if its work is done in secret, without the play of conscious reflection.

And yet, there is another sense, or at least, an extent to which, we are not obliged to "choose" between these two alterna-tives. For in a sense they are not truly alternatives; at least, not so mutually exclusive as I have (following the Death-of-God theologies, and Karl Adam himself) all too brutally presented them.

We are not, I submit, obliged to reject, as so much "idolatry," contemporary man's conviction of the relative autonomy of created causes; the reality of creaturely being and activity that St. Thomas so determinedly championed. These things really do exist, and are fully equipped by the Creator to act, and act in accordance with their natures.

This was the fundamental stance of Thomism that author-ized Copleston to observe that Aquinas actually furnished modern science with its basic epistemological and metaphysical charter of legitimacy: if one wishes to know how things behave, one must begin with careful observation, carefully systematized.

And the scientific constructs that emerge from that process cannot be simply tossed off as "idolatry": the total human subject who both believes and understands cannot live in some schizophrenic world where belief and understanding do not come into some significant rhyme.

The fideism Vahanian calls us to, then, is no solution—or better, it is a solution we have seen too often in history, and each time come to reject. Its counterpart is a kind of quietistic trust in God that places man in the supine position of total inertia: the cuddling religion of infancy, childish rather than childlike, that the secular city theologian rightly repudiates. "Pray as if everything depended on God; act as if everything depended on you": so runs the all-too familiar misquotation from St. Ignatius Loyola. But Ignatius said a sounder, and profounder thing: one not nearly so flat and obvious as that. And what he really said places us once again before our problem squarely but at its deepest level. "Pray," he said, "knowing everything depends upon you; act, knowing everything depends upon God." What is rejected on the one hand is the complete Pelagianism of action that the secular world would draw us to, but on the other hand, Ignatius just as firmly rejects the quietistic reliance on God that would sap the springs of action.

Instead of having to choose between these two versions of the world, then, his apothegm advises us we must find some deeper level at which those versions can be brought into some sort of harmony. This harmony will never be facile or obvious; it will never eliminate the truth that the atmosphere of the Christian's relation both with God and world is always one; as St. Thomas loved to remind his readers, of mystery: *omnia exeunt in mysterium.*

But if that be true, then we can never claim to have arrived at some final and definitive, ultimately satisfying resolution of the problem. If that were necessary, then only the greatest of theologians could feel that, on the basis of his confident solution, he could finally get on to the business of praying. If the Christian community had to leave prayer to its theologians, we might be in a pretty fix indeed! And yet, if the Christian community were not dimly aware that somewhere in the theological sector of that Christian community, there was being formulated at least the adumbration of a solution to the problem, then its faith—and prayer—would inevitably suffer. Not die, mind you, but find itself truncated, lamed, to a greater or lesser extent schizophrenic.

V. "POINTING THE WAY"

I can claim no more than the ability and intention to suggest some adumbration of a solution. For this is all that is necessary, and is quite sufficient to our purposes here. "Not to be told, not to be spoken of," the great Plotinus warned of old to those who wanted quick recipes for the ascent his philosophy promised them. "We can but point the way, indicate the path."

But there is hope in the fact that the way in question has frequently been marked, the path is well-trodden. Again and again it has been pointed out (and by scientists, among others) that for all its pragmatic value, for all its signal triumphs, the version of our world here denominated as "scientific" remains partial and inadequate. What it tells may be true, but once one properly situates the language of its telling, one realizes that it is not the whole truth, nor can it ever claim to be. To take the scientific version of our world as the whole truth about that world would involve us, in Whitehead's phrase, in the "fallacy of misplaced concreteness"—of taking an abstract skeleton of reality for the full-bodied, fleshed and fully-complected concrete.

The inadequacy of this (older) scientific view becomes all the more apparent when one fixes on the privileged style of thought that figured so prominently in its method: the mathematical. To again use a metaphor of Whitehead, a style of thought is as important to the scientific endeavor as Ophelia is to Shakespeare's *Hamlet*—and yet, like Ophelia, charming and beautiful and faintly mad. Twenty-five hundred years ago, Plato wrote the *Parmenides* to query (as I understand him) how the *dianoetic* type of thought exercised in the mathematics he had become so fond of could be brought into unison with the soaring kind of insight that brought him to his vision of the Good, the One, the Beautiful. The question, I submit, is with us today still: and the answer is still *not* a unilateral adoption of, and trust in, the mathematical cast of thinking. There are more things in life than are dreamt of, at least, by *that* kind of philosophizing.

It is instructive in this regard to remind ourselves of how often in history the tyranny of one kind of thinking has provoked the violent resurgence of its opposite style of thought: how the Romantics in the nineteenth century stood up to a man to tell us that the world was more sinuous, more richly textured, more mysterious and charged with divine intimations, than the conquering Newtonians were prepared to admit. There are, they said, other ways of perceiving, richer modes of assimilating the fullness of reality—poetic, symbolic, esthetic, mystical modes— that must be brought simultaneously to bear, if our view of the world is not to become lamentably impoverished. "There dwells the dearest freshness deep down things" that it would be tragic for a human being not to catch glimpses of. At the end of his analytic tether, Wittgenstein seems to shrug his shoulders wearily while admitting that for all the rigor of his method, there remain things about which our ordinary styles of declarative speech seem condemned to silence; and one of them reminds us of Heiddegger's throbbing question: when science has started with the world that exists, and explained its working to us forward and backward, upward and downward, we are still left with the question that brings all the resources of other styles of thought back into play: why should there be anything at all?

But can science pretend even to have explained the reality we know, as it understands the term explanation? One can doubt it. For there is one feature of our world where science regularly boggles, the feature the ancient mythologist claimed was primary: the person. We have, Teilhard was brought to protest (and he knew far more about this than some have imagined), as yet no science to embrace our entire world, from atom to man.

And man, the person, is as massive and compelling a phenomenon as the order of the physical universe. If one were to choose between them, indeed, which is the more compelling fact? Teilhard's answer is clear: his way of spelling out that answer may have gaps, but the tendency of his thought strikes me as offering more than merely an adumbration: it offers us a way of fully appreciating the scientific view at its proper worth, and yet, completing and integrating it into a more comprehensive mode of "seeing" that once again unmasks our universe and reveals it as disclosing both a heart and a face. A universe as Personal. A universe in which the wonder that there is anything at all is coupled with the surprise that what appear as deterministic modes of action, mathematically graphed and plotted, really, on inspection, dissolve into a myriad of swarming spontaneities. A Divine Milieu in which we bathe at every point of our being, an atmosphere sustaining *both* our prayer *and* our action—a world which, on examination, once again strangely resembles the universe as Jesus viewed it, in which he prayed and acted, to which he entrusted himself unreservedly, with the sweet confidence of a child that could face the death it brought him and reply: "Father, into thy hands I commend my spirit."

Notes

[1] Karl Adam, *The Son of God* (New York, 1932). The quotations that follow appear on pp. 142-145.

[2] Gabriel Vahanian, *The Death of God* (New York, 1957).

[3] Cf. Thomas J. J. Altizer and William Hamilton, *Radical Theology and the Death of God* (New York, 1966); Paul M. Van Buren, *The Secular Meaning of the Gospel* (New York, 1963); Harvey Cox, *The Secular City* (New York, 1965).

[4] Leslie Dewart, *The Future of Belief* (New York, 1966).

[5] Alfred North Whitehead, *Science and the Modern World* (New York, Mentor edition, 1968). It is important to acknowledge that many of the facets of the Newtonian worldview Whitehead criticizes have since been modified by scientists themselves. The theological difficulties being handled here arise, however, from the fact that residues of the older view still hang on, at least in the popular mind.

intercession, sympathy, and the eschaton

JULIAN N. HARTT

The first part of this essay presents three theses concerning intercessory prayer. The second part of the paper has itself two parts: the first is an analysis of sympathy as a precondition of intercessory prayer; the second is an interpretation of sympathy as an objective or "destiny" of intercession. In the last part I have attempted to show that sympathy conceived as the destiny of intercession is qualitatively different from sympathy as a precondition. It follows from this that intercession must be protected against the wrong kind of "eschatological invasion." Eschatological heightening of cultural crisis may accentuate the place of intercession. But it may also obscure the position of intercession in the Kingdom of Glory.

I.

A. Intercession is the supreme mode of prayer.

The force of "supreme" is simply "preeminent." It does not argue proprietory rights or authority to subsume other modes of prayer under itself. I do not intend to develop here the relations of intercession to the other modes of prayer.

Of what consists the preeminence of intercession in the prayers of the Christian and of the Church? Of this primarily, that it shows forth the incarnational presence of God and man with each other in that perfection of sympathy which grace alone supplies.

John 17 is the paradigm for the intercessory prayers of the Christian because it is the supreme representation of the intercessory life of the Incarnate Lord. Here Christ does indeed "stand between" man and God. He does indeed "plead a case" —that of the disciples first and thereafter for "those who are to believe in me through their word."

Surely it is worthy of note that Christ the Lord does nothing to threaten the integrity of the human situation in and for which he expresses divine concern. He does not as God and for God preempt every human power, leaving only God to transact something with himself. Jesus Christ so *prays* for his chosen that he stands actually in their place to represent their interests

99

before the throne of God the Father. His beneficiaries are not thereby relieved of the harsh necessity of living and working in a world bitterly hostile to them. He does not intend that his intercession should change the world for their benefit. He asks of the Father that these men may be sanctified for the sake of the divine work of redemption in the world.

Thus the imitation of Christ is given wonderfully rich content. The Christian and the Church are called and potentialized to replicate the intercession of the Lord Christ.

"Replication" is of course not entirely adequate as a description of this calling because it carries a hint of a mechanical kind of duplication; whereas in fact nothing could be less mechanical than the participative life to which we are called in Jesus Christ. This explains part of the hostility of the "world." Christian existence is projected beyond the security and good sense of legalistic rules. It is therefore projected also beyond what the "world" calls freedom. These offenses are amplified by the intercessions of Church and Christian: Christ's people persist in praying that the "world" will seek the higher righteousness and freedom.

We should not doubt that other modes of prayer are indispensable in Christian discipleship. Nor should we doubt that another prayer may be more fundamental. Further reflection on John 17 may persuade us that if we are to be active agents in intercession we must already be endowed with the higher gifts of grace. Much seems already to have been determined; and especially readiness to follow Christ in life and death for the glory of the kingdom. To those who needed fundamental instruction in prayer so as to avoid the meaningless repetitions of the heathen, Jesus Christ taught quite a different prayer. That prayer has (if we may dare to say so) a considerable amount of self-referencing to the persons praying. "Give *us* this day *our* daily bread." "Forgive *us our* trespasses." Where is "Give bread to those who need it much more than we do"? Or, "Forgive all who need to be forgiven"? In response it is proper to say that *that* praying for others is in principle settled in "Thy kingdom come, thy will be done, on earth as it is in heaven." Would to

God that were true in fact! The Lord's Prayer has long since been established in our prayer life as a routine barely distinguishable from "vain repetition"; and if it does come to life in any part, that part is likely to be an impassioned plea that our bread not be intercepted by lawless elements in our society.

I do not feel constrained to soften this accusation. Nevertheless it is only fair to concede that there is considerable merit buried in the naive view that the prayer for the kingdom "in principle" controls an excessive display of self-concern in "Give us our daily bread." What is that merit? It is simply the fact that being possessed by a holy concern for others does not either in principle or in fact wait upon a radical overturning or upending of self-interest. Indeed the actuality of the moral as such confronts us here. Concern for the well-being of others is what the moral claim is about; and to get on with what one does not need to prescind from self-concern. It is also true that to get on with the moral business one must learn to put oneself in the place of others, one must learn both to feel for others and to feel as others feel. These are two quite different modes of fellow feeling or sympathy. In Part II further attention will be paid to the distinction. It is noted here as a detail of the first thesis. No legitimate interpretation of that thesis runs in the direction of a claim that in intercession grace overrides nature. Intercession reveals how grace *penetrates* nature, modulating the forms and energies of the natural life toward a destiny adumbrated in the moral claim but not in the natural course of events consummated there.

B. The objective of intercession is penetration of a human state of affairs by divine grace.

Every faithful prayer is a *prayer for,* having unfailingly (in principle) an objective. Thus even contemplative prayer is ordered to an end. Christ calls no one to lose all reliable sense of self, world and God in holy meditation. In his name we ought to resist every proposal—religious or otherwise—to diminish consciousness, or conversely, to heighten it to the (illusory) point wherein self, world and God merge, become one.

The direct target of the penetration prayed for is a state of affairs. We pray for people in a concrete situation. I suppose most of us think well of the spiritual generosity which disposes us to pray indeterminately for people in general no matter what their situations might be—"God bless mummy, daddy, Aunt Sallie, Father O'Sullivan, Rover and baby sister," a descending order of priorities. We do not normally advise the child to wait and see what fix any of her beneficiaries is in before launching her bedtime prayer, though I am not sure why we do not. It just might make her prayers significantly different from other routines, such as brushing her golden tresses and her crooked teeth. Spiritual generosity is a beautiful thing but it can slip away into lack of focus upon concrete persons, human beings defined for all practical purposes by the horizons of a particular time, place and good-and-evil.

The point at issue can be put somewhat more contentiously. Persons in situations, rather than metaphysical substances, are the objectives of intercession. What is presented for penetration by divine grace is a finite moral agent confronted with choices; but the grace of God is not to be represented as a missile bearing in on armor plate. To the extent that "penetration" betokens that kind of action, it is wrong. "Participation" in that case is nearer the mark. Divine grace is to be represented as an agent among other agents in a field of action rather than as an invisible force invading the inner being of some of the agents, capturing them for the glory of the eternal kingdom, or reducing them to spiritual particles dancing gratefully in the Son-beams of Heaven.

No doubt there are theological oddities in this second thesis; or at least in the construction placed on that thesis by these latter comments. I suspect that some of these oddities attend every serious interpretation of the prayers of the Christian and the Church. One such oddity stands out above the others, the strange business of a creature *asking* God to do either what God does without invitation or what no invitation could induce him to do. Some philosophers have been scandalized by *any* petitionary prayer, believing that the practitioner of such prayer is bound to falsify either himself or God by anything that goes beyond praise and meditation. Let your praying—if pray you must—*celebrate* something rather than bend dignity and plausibility out of shape by seeking to alter or ch..nge something. That is solemn philosophic counsel.

Why do we not more carefully heed it? Not, I think, because the now dominant policy in philosophical circles runs against trying to reform human behavior. A better reason is itself almost philosophical: We cannot take very seriously counsel springing from a profoundly inaccurate conception of the actualities. The intercessor in Christ is assuredly not trying to induce God to do what he does without induction, nor is he putting God up to doing something he cannot or will not do. Rather, in his faithful prayer the Christian participates in a life God graciously shares with man for the knitting-up of the human condition into the "likeness" of its creator.

I do not mean to suggest that the participational life of intercession casts a destructive shadow over every element of externality in the relation of creator to creature. If the divine creative act does indeed spring from the divine aseity, and in no respect compromises or reduces it, then we can and must continue to speak of God as being "out there" and "over against us" as well as "self-complete from all eternity." But when we apprehend redemption and sanctification as the work of the Incarnate Lord, the last element of externality cries out for redemption. Thanks to Jesus Christ man does not need to obey a God whose commandments are dark, whose purpose is inscrutable, and whose *modus operandi* is caprice. All of these alienating powers have been taken captive by Christ. This being so, man does not need to obey a secret inner self that miraculously retains its purity no matter how bloody the course it dictates for the outer world.

Intercession is the triumphant expression of the participational life. In the paradigm case, John 17, the requests Christ makes of the Father radiate an intimacy of mutual knowledge, love and trust that obliges us to reconceive what we want to say and can say about internal and external relationships. The Father and the Son are united in a common will. This means that there is a common good each intends distinctively as the very definition of his being.

The doctrine of the Trinity no doubt abounds with metaphysical puzzles, though these are hardly the products of pure metaphysical speculation. Given magisterial texts such as John 17, trinitarian thinking is constrained to find concepts and images with which to express the immense and palpable mystery of the Divine Persons "penetrating" one another without the slightest hint of any preemption of the being and authority of one by any other or by any concert of the others. It would be odd indeed to say that the three Persons occupy a situation to which each makes his distinctive response. It would not be so odd to say that the absolute goodness of being establishes the horizons within which all dwell together in the highest perfection of sympathy.

Such sympathy, such an intimacy of mutual knowledge, love and trust is both presupposed and radiated by the intercession of the Son, Jesus Christ. In what follows now particular attention will be paid to the presupposing of sympathy. In his intercession Christ the Son creates a human state of affairs in which the Father's love is triumphantly revealed as the ground-condition of all that exists; and it is therefore the foundation upon which Christ creates the new order of existence, through his intercessory life.

C. Sympathy is a necessary precondition for the divine-human transaction of intercession.

This thesis may seem hopelessly extravagant. From a simple psychological fact—people must care about others if they are truly to intercede for them—an astounding theological claim is hurled outward into an implausible empyrean. "What, you dare suggest that *anything* in heaven or earth is a necessary precondition for divine intercession!" If we persist in that line we shall be likely to start drawing weird pictures of God having first in his own being to lay down a foundation of sympathy, then in Jesus Christ and thereafter in others, before the great work of intercession can commence.

I am no readier than the next one to encourage that kind of theological-poetic license. The third thesis ought therefore to be hedged about to prevent that. For that purpose it may help to keep before us the view of intercession as a divine-human transaction in which each of the high contracting parties is (or in man's case, becomes) fully himself in the very situation of greatest public expenditure of his being to secure the well-being of others.

Here the decisive word is "transaction." We may be tempted at this point to fall back on "encounter" as a fair synonym; but it is no more satisfactory than "confrontation." "Encounter" has too much of the fortuitous about it—"can you guess whom I encountered on the way to the fair?" "Confrontation" carries too much of the showdown of hostile dominions—"we will confront the administration." What we are after is a term for the intentional convergence of two beings each of which is fully alive to the value of the other, and gives himself therefore to the enhancement ("glorification") of the other. Furthermore this occurs in a state of affairs populated with neutral factors some of which are human beings who do not sense their own stake in the transaction. This does not make them creatures of demonic callousness. Who has not learned from experience, or from art, that great events do not always *feel* great in their occurrence? Moreover, some of the divine-human transactions to which the New Testament bears witness produced no visible or measurable change in the state of affairs which housed them. The nearby world, to say nothing of the far-flung, went on unheeding.

Yet we strongly resist the supposition that divine-human transactions leave the native setting unaltered. Why? Perhaps we also learn from experience that truly momentous events on the plains of human history do make all kinds of differences in the nearby and far-flung world. Some of this impact is intentional, some of it is fortuitous; but it is felt at the time; and discerning spirits sense the shifting of the world. *A fortiori* any event in which God is present is certain to be even more inclusive and decisive in its revolutionary impact.

The matter is perplexing. On the one hand we have reason to believe that divine-human transactions may not be "historic" at all—may not, that is, alter forthwith the visible face of the world or leave large marks on the public record of mankind. Gethsemene, for example. Romantic imagination portrays that as the formidable darkness in which the fate of the Roman Empire is sealed and the world-historical process is therefore obliged to lunge in a different direction.

Whatever its poetic power such a representation of Gethsemene takes more instruction from aesthetic license than from history. There is no tough evidence that the decisive character of this transaction was sensed at the time by anyone other than the principal actor. Slowly and fragmentarily the true import of the event—its shape, potency and direction—is apprehended. Thus in due time the decisive import of Gethsemene is faithfully registered. It was the transaction in which the destiny of a community is made finally and absolutely to coalesce with the vocation of a man. From this moment forward there will be no turning back, no renunciation of that vocation, no denying that destiny; not because irresistible forces had long since been set in motion; but because God and the man of his own choosing have bound themselves together in an unalterable covenant, pledge and promise.

We can, of course, speculate metaphysically or lyrically. Perhaps even then Jesus Christ could have changed his mind; or better yet, God, now wholly convinced that he had in this man Jesus the highest possible perfection of the Isaac spirit— that spirit of utter trust in a Father who has inexplicably donned the mask of executioner—might have stayed the execution and allowed the quondam victim to enter the rabbinate in Nazareth, a onetime revolutionary sobered by a very close call. Poetic fantasies of this sort are probably no more depressing than theological flights so heavily loaded with metaphysical equipment that they can only bustle up and down the runways roaring enviously at their poetic cousins winging off toward blue horizons far away. But happy the age which does not need to look to either for salvation!

If we have lost the scent of that happiness we ought not to blame either God or our fathers. We may have prized too highly certain philosophical assurances that all of the meaning of the divine-human transaction was *there* all of the time; and needed only the proper instruments, themselves the gift of Providence or Holy Spirit, to refine and solidify it into nuggets of immortal gold. Why must the past be so rich, the present so poor, the future so bound? An honest answer is not likely to flatter, it will glorify God only at our expense.

I suggest that an explanation of sympathy may help again to put intercession where it belongs both in our theology and in prayers, that is as the most luminous co-presence of God and man.

What we mean by sympathy is a penetration, via the mode of feeling, of the situation of an other person. Intercession for the other is abortive, even though well-intentioned, if it does not spring from sympathy; for then the interceding act does not operate with the actualities. Efficacious intercession operates with the actual condition of the other—actual, not illusory. In addition, to be efficacious intercession must operate with the actual condition of the *intercessor*. This means that efficacy of intercession presupposes an openness in the initiator to the reciprocal plunge of sympathy. I may not need what I ask for the other—though of course I can be quite mistaken about that. But in any case the other must have my unstinted compliance in his indispensable effort to discern who I am in my concern for him: friend? imperialist? self-hater . . . ? If intercession is to become efficacious the intercessor must forswear every interest in covering his tracks. He must retain his own integrity of being. That means he must eschew concealment, that pseudo-mystery into which we are all tempted to flee the light of truth.

It does not follow that *disinterestedness* is incompatible with sympathy. The moral life can boast few more beautiful achievements than this wonderful and fragile virtue. But it is not qualified to be the supreme ruler in the moral life—it is best understood and sought as monitor rather than as emperor. Thus sympathy ought to survive and even flourish in company with disinterestedness; for what is that quality if it is not the ability (or at least the desire) to tell clearly the difference between one's own interests and the interests of another, and thereafter to act upon that perception. If this difference were always or necessarily that of contradiction or irreconciliability then sympathy could hardly survive a heavy application of disinterestedness; but that is not the case. Quite to the contrary, sympathy comes into its own when the I refuses to make any self-referencing feeling or passion the sufficient motive for seeking the real good of the actual other. This does not represent a flight from passion. Through the miracle of disinterestedness the contours and perimeters of a passion are amplified to include the I and the other in a "higher synthesis."

What then can take the place of sympathy as a motive in intercession? Not duty. The duty to pray for others is so heavily laid upon us, early and late, by priest and other parental figures, that we can hardly imagine ourselves doing it without the sense of duty. Truly, we have no quarrel with that as a conditioning factor: we cannot trust ourselves spontaneously to obey God and seek the best for our brethren. But when the duty to pray for others is so heavily laid on we can confidently expect that the only joy derived from the performance will be self-satisfaction, the steady pursuit of which does not carry us toward the kingdom of God.

Yet taken as a motive sympathy could lead us to construe intercession as a move calculated to extract the I and the other from a painful common predicament: I want you to be relieved of your suffering because so long as you are in and I am sympathetic, I must share it. No doubt this experience is common enough, but that must not lead us to think it normative or unavoidable. For in fact I may not intercede for your suffering to cease. I may ask God to give you grace that something affirmative for others may be made from your suffering. If I am properly sympathetic I want something more and better than an early end to your suffering. I want for you a greater "power of being" and particularly a greater responsiveness to the existence and potentialities of others. So we do not pray primarily for the curtain of suffering to lift, even though there are days and nights when we could not imagine or crave a better thing. We pray that even the harshest vicissitude will not stifle the creative spirit. There is actually no choice but to *pray* for that, but not because we have been stripped of every other power. A simple unalterable fact confronts us here: creativity of spirit cannot be imposed or transmitted, it arises from the mysterious depths of being where the boundaries between self and everlastingly fecund grace are elastic. Accordingly intercessory prayer is the remote but real analogy of the movement of grace in the depths luring the creative act out into the open abounding life. Grace knows nothing of coercion. Therefore intercession is not a "power play." Grace does not practice the arts of seduction. Therefore intercession eschews them. Prayer, thus, is not abdication or despair of power. It is the expression of a great and holy desire to be open to grace as the power of God.

Sympathy carries us toward the interior center of the other. That is why we say it is a necessary precondition for the divine-human transaction of intercession. The grace of God is oblivious to the boundaries of creaturely selfhood. Yet God does nothing to destroy those boundaries—indeed he has created them. God is thus himself as grace that very sympathy upon which the intercessory life is posited; and as such it is no achievement of ours. Yet there is a sympathy that we intend as an attainment within our capability.

In the second part of this paper some light may be thrown on this situation by developing the distinction between "feeling for" and "feeling as." With this in hand we may be able to make more of the distinction between sympathy as precondition and sympathy as an objective of intercession.

II.

The ordinary expression, "I am feeling for you" is full of oddities. It will be useful to consider some of these.

A. The force of *for* in "I am feeling for you" may be *in your place,* as when one says, "I am voting your proxy"; as though the other were incapable of feeling for himself.

B. But *for* may also signify that one is searching for the other. "I am feeling for you" in that case can be translated as "Where are you? I am trying to find you"; something like "Since I am in the dark I must feel for the lightswitch."

C. When one says, "I have a feeling for you" something still different is intended, something like "I have a feeling, or a certain feeling, for Stravinsky or Braque or Wallace Stevens"; and this in turn is apparently translatable as "I dig it." Thus feeling-for here signifies an affinity deeper than mere taste. In personal relationships this affinity is called rapport. Rapport is a feeling-state. It may well include shared aims; but the mode of sharing is feeling.

D. Feeling-for is a primitive valuation, well on the way to the grammatical ellision of the preposition "for," as in the expression, "Man, I really *feel* that." This calls attention to something more than rapport or affinity. Here "feel" signifies an immediacy and richness of participation in a good thing; or if not automatically a good thing as object, then at least the mode of presentation of the object is good because it admits of academic doubt only; thus, "once you have really *felt* it (whatever it is) you really *know* it."

Sympathy as a natural primordial fact is very like some modes of *feeling-for.* Man is endowed with a capacity for fellow-feeling. This testifies to the wisdom of his creator, surely. Human life can therefore be sensibly construed as a high order organism having a nervous system uniting every cell and particle. I may not *want* to feel what is going on elsewhere in the system; but I have to work to prevent it; and the effort may be futile. One does well to be wary of taking this to mean that I feel identically what is going on in you, if I but give sympathy its head. That kind of penetration of the other calls for a highly developed imagination, among other things. That is why we say it is an achievement rather than a primordial element. At the primordial level we pick off feelings in the air—for example, in a snob. But we do not know on that level how any particular person is feeling, how he has interiorized the situation. That calls for powers the situation suppresses.

How does *feeling-for* throw light on sympathy as a primordial fact? Let us experiment.

1. "You have my sympathy" may mean "I know how immobilized you are by suffering; but *I* am not immobilized by that fact. So in your place and in your behalf I am feeling things you apparently cannot for the time being feel—the beauty of hope in a great tomorrow."

If this seems wildly fanciful let me remind you that we frequently assure others seized by paroxysms of pain that "sometime you'll understand why." Taken one way this is grossly impertinent and empirically wrong to boot; that is, as a prediction that a necessary and sufficient explanation of the problem of suffering will sometime occur to them. Viewed quite differently the odium vanishes, that is as a reminder that well within the perimeters of the other's life there is a replenishment of hope. I bespeak that when I say, therefore, "I feel for you." Sympathy here moves within shared perimeters; and reaches out for promised sustenance.

2. Primordial sympathy also has something of the element of search for a missing but real presence. Unlike the situation envisaged by (1), here I share the dark with you. I must enter the dark to find you since you are in the dark. I am not God, so I cannot banish this inclusive darkness by the simple fiat, "Let there be light!" This does not mean I must therefore be as lost as you. What would be the virtue in coming in after you if by that I too lost all touch with the light and peace of home? Both of us swallowed up by common darkness we could comfort each other by calling out, "Over here!" but nothing would be "over here" except a particular condensation of confusion, terror and despair.

But even if I am in touch with home as I seek you there is a good deal of randomness and uncertainty in store for me. I must feel here, I must feel there. I am receiving your signals but they are erratic and fragmentary, and perhaps hermetic as well. Our common situation is further complicated by the signals I send as the darkness begins to oppress me—anxiety, uncertainty, frustration. Sympathy has induced me to feel you out. Sympathy alone will not provide a solid contact with you and thereafter a sure exit from darkness for both of us.

3. and 4. Sympathy is a rudimentary valuation placed upon (or read off) the other. So sympathetic response is more than a shared predicament, shared actually or imaginatively. Sympathy is also an appreciation of the other in that situation. The other is more than a target for a rescue operation—ah, how nice! We have the rescue equipment and now we have someone to use it on! The other is a value in his own right. His value is a prime explanation for our decision to intercede. We may bring to this decision an unalterable conviction that gratuitous suffering anywhere, anybody's ought to be eliminated. But the good of interceding for the concrete other is not a deduction from a general metaphysical-ethical rule. Sympathy as feeling-for has carried the I into the situation of the other. The prime value of now acting to resolve that situation is a function of *his* value. This does not mean that the I consistently makes a greater effort for a particular other than for the rest of creation or of mankind though this is often enough the case. It does mean that efficacious intercession is sympathetic effort proportioned to the concrete person. That is why a feeling-for the "special case," as each creature under God is, is so important. And that is why we admire the person who knows just what to do, not merely because of years of rigorous discipline but because of his astute perception of *this* person in *this* situation.

What then is to be made of "feeling as," or, to follow vulgar usage for the moment, "feeling like" as in "I feel like you do"?

This expression seems to describe the kind of identity of self and other denied or not attained by "feeling-for." For now one appears to be saying something very like "I have the same feeling you have," which suggests that there is one feeling with two subjects, I at this end and you at the other.

This gives us a very strong meaning for "sympathy" namely a shared feeling rather than a shared situation, shared aims or shared history. And this is surely more than a "feeling-with." The feeling is now yours and mine; and perhaps others as well have it identically.

Several things ought to be said about this account of sympathy. One: characteristically it is a claim or a testimony offered for feeling that has made it up into the category of *passion*. Second: this means that the valuation involved has risen above triviality and randomness into massiveness and necessity. Third: as passion it is something which has us rather than we have it—we profess to be grasped by it.

But if these observations are sound, what is left to the proposal that sympathy in this mode is an achievement rather than a primordial element? For sympathy to become the passion of identity primitive fellow-feeling must be transmuted by imagination, desire and will. It is not one of the dictates of nature that we should simply fall into this kind of rapport, this kind of identity. This pertains to destiny, not to fate. Destiny is a part of the language of intention.

Intercession (intercessory prayer) presupposes sympathy as the capacity for *feeling-for* the other. Intercession has a primary objective in the achievement of sympathy as *feeling-as*. Sympathy in the latter sense is the destiny of intercession.

This proposal is not intended, incidentally, to be an escape from the question: Does intercession make any changes in the "objective situation"? It is not, that is, a proposal to look upon "subjective" change as the real—though not always the intended —achievement of intercession. Intercession certainly looks toward the modification of human subjects; but not simply toward modification of their feelings, if we suppose feeling is a private internal affair. We need not so regard feeling. We do not need to suppose that feeling is any more private than any other element of experience. Much confusion on this is generated by failure to distinguish between something that *occurs* only on the inside from something that is likely to be read one way from the inside out and read another way from the outside in. But that is a matter of *evaluating* an experience rather than a matter of *having* it. If I insist that my pain is mine in some exclusive sense, I err. If I say that it "means" something to me it is not likely to mean to you, that makes good sense; but its import is that I must try to *do* something about it that you are *not* obligated to do. When my tooth hurts I ought to see the dentist. It is good of you to say "I know how you feel," but that feeling-knowledge of yours certainly does not set you off to find the dentist—though if you are sympathetic enough I may ask you to go with me to hold my hand or pay the bill.

Sympathy as destiny rather than as a simple fact of nature (fate) looks toward a situation in which self and other shall share both feeling and obligation to act the same way upon it, for it and with it. Intercessory prayer is an adumbration of that kind of participation in a common life. Intercession here and now means bearing one another's burdens. It looks toward a time and a world in which the burden of one is actually *felt* by all. That is sympathy raised to a new level of perception, responsiveness and efficacy. That is sympathy infused with grace whose grand and glorious intention has been plainly disclosed. The natural fact of sympathy does not unlock that intention. The key for that is a gift of God the Holy Spirit, a sympathy bound out for an identity of self and other only dimly adumbrated in the best moments of our natural loving.

The ability and willingness actually to feel what the other is feeling is part of the efficacy for which intercession is destined. No doubt we begin by supposing that *that* is not the way history is made, worlds lost and won. It does not smack of creativity on a large scale.

The supposition is partly wrong and partly inappropriate. Divine-human transactions do not have as their intentional objective the making or the remaking of world history. They are focused upon the plight of this soul and that soul. They look not toward world empire but to the reclamation of whomever and whatever of God's creation is lost in darkness. In his sovereign wisdom and power God may use such small obscure events as drops of water out of which to compose a vast ocean. That is his business, his alone.

Thus intercession has a primary objective in the coming of

grace into the control center of human life in a concrete situation. This is something to be prayed for because God ordains and employs this transaction to that end. It is footless speculation to wonder whether God might not be able to accomplish that end otherwise. The end in view is a community in which each cares enough to give himself for the blessing of the other, and knows through the immediacies of feeling where and how the other is. Rarely do we have now that kind of feeling. For the larger part we have to make up for the errancy and confusions of feeling with goodness of intention and resolution of will. That is why in intercession we pray obliquely for ourselves. How greatly do our feelings need to be honed on the grindstones of actuality! How careful we are to respect the boundaries of the other, for fear that in retaliation—however loving—our own might be pierced! We do not, in good faith, allow these things to rise to the top of the agenda for intercession. But God knows them for what they are. The transaction into which he summons us will do something about them. "Brethren, it does not yet appear what we shall become. . . . But we know that we shall become like him" who continually offers intercession for us at the throne of grace.

III.

The sympathy into which we are called in Jesus Christ, who for our achievement of the same offers intercession, is not the sympathy with which we enter into that relationship. The primordial element is not abolished or defaced. It is transformed beyond anything we could do for ourselves. Yet this does not occur outside of us and our situation. Nothing so becomes our being and our lot. Nothing is less likely to be done by ourselves alone.

In this concluding section I want to present two supplemental proposals. The first: The intercessory life in Christ is a new synthesis (ontologically new) of action and passion. The second: It is a mistake to look for an eschatological overcoming of sympathy, and thus of intercession, in the Kingdom of God.

Christianity long ago assimilated from classical Greek

thought a formidable axiom, compact of ontological and ethical intuitions. *It is better to act than to be acted upon.* This axiom warrants, perhaps inspires, representations of the divine life of highest perfection as unalloyed and self-sustaining activity immune to the slightest hint of passivity.

There is an equally famous corollary. *Feeling belongs to passivity; and passion is the supreme case of passivity.* Again, the corollary licenses, and perhaps inspires, certain representations of the good man as the one whose rational control of his passion makes him a proper reflection of the highest God, who has no passions. Thus the good man maintains distance from his fellows.

It must be said that Christian theologians have done remarkably little to liberate Christian life from bondage to these pagan axioms, despite the fact that neither the revelation of God in Jesus Christ nor the model of the good man derived from that is compatible with them. Largely without the assistance of theologians we are coming to see that passion is not an imperfection, either in man or in his Creator. This being so it behooves us to redo the ancient distinction between the higher and the lower passions. It will not do to make the criterion freedom from the "bodily bias" so that the higher are more "spiritual" and the lower more sensate. The criterion called for is *lucidity of intentional object.* The lower passions are not lower because of proximity to the "physical." Some passions will settle for anything in a class of objects. That makes them lower than a passion for a concrete determinate being. Some feelings are largely self-referencing. That makes them lower than feelings that intend existence other than the self.

Sympathy is a passion. No passion has a greater potentiality for carrying us to the heights of activity concentrated upon the good. For this to happen, something must happen to sympathy. That is the transformation of sympathy in intercession from a natural fact into a feature of the ultimate destiny of the creature at the hands of divine grace. Thus emerges a new ontological synthesis of action and passion. The New Testament term for this is "the new creature." The Johannine expression for it is

"sanctification," as in John 17. Far from being lifted beyond
the realm of passion by the sanctifying presence, the man of
faith suffers an immense increase of passion. He is miraculously
sensitized to the value of life in its myriad forms and awful
predicaments. His capacities for suffering are thus enormously
augmented. He can *will* to become part of suffering anywhere,
since the mind of Christ does indeed indwell his mortal frame.

This grace-ful (wrought by grace) power to feel is part of
the enhancement of the self's capabilities of action. The sanctified are precisely those who can now "do the perfect will of God."
No longer need they struggle against counter-tendencies and
fatal irresolution in themselves. As they are moved by feelings
of great vividness and lucidity, so they act with bounding energy
and wonderful simplicity. What they have a feeling for they now
find resources to initiate, sustain and complete. No longer need
they struggle with an overpowering sense of the futility of every
effort made to mitigate insurmountable evil. God will use
their faithful intercessions to overcome that evil, in his own time
and in his own way. To the "saints" he gives the supreme
assurance: They have not prayed in vain.

But if such is the high calling which we have in Christ
Jesus, it would seem to adumbrate the eschatological abolition
of intercession in the Kingdom of God; and this for two immediate reasons. (a) Once the self is sufficiently imbued with
sanctifying grace to act efficaciously in behalf of others, the
need for sympathy is abolished, sympathy that is as feeling the
sufferings of others. For if I can actually do something about
your plight I am excused from not feeling very badly about it.
(b) When the kingdom of man has been taken up into the
glory of the divine kingdom there will be no need of intercession;
for by scriptural promise there will be no night there, neither
tears nor sighing.

(a) This presupposes that vital elements of their distinctive
creaturehood have been removed from the sanctified. It preserves,
as well, the ancient prejudice against passion. To the first of
these conjoint errors we ought again to say that nothing more
ennobles man than his capacity to participate in the suffering

of others, whether or not that suffering, judged on some purely human scale, is deserved. (This of course is to be distinguished from sentimental self-indulgence, since in that condition the self loves its own feelings more than anything else.) Therefore we cannot properly even imagine a situation in which the self can be relieved of that capacity and still retain its power to act efficaciously in behalf of others. Sympathy as destiny is an indispensable expression of human solidarity in creation, guilt, redemption and sanctification.

Perhaps a brief comment upon "efficacy" will provide a sensible transition to the refutation of the second eschatological error.

The natural bent of man is to act well rather than merely to be doing something. That is a passing good reason for knowing what we mean by a natural preference for action over passivity; for we are prone to confuse *action* with *movement*. A person cerebrating furiously over a problem is surely acting; but he may be rooted in one spot from dusk to dawn, except for the exigencies of the flesh—and even those may get short shrift until the case is solved. So the sole virtue of the notion of *movement* in this connection is its hint of transaction in the public world. We do not *act* except in the public world. The force of "public" is not "in fact observed by x number of other perceivers" but "a state of affairs susceptible of being so modified by one constituent (agent) of it that *any* number of other constituents must take that modification into account in taking that state of affairs into account." All that means is that action is difference-making, where the difference can be described in terms recognizable to any number of agents, whether or not in fact any such agent admits that such a difference has been made.

Thus the natural desire to be efficacious in action is the desire to effect a significant change. It does not matter for this argument *how* significant or significant for how many.

Let us return now to (b) above: If I can really *do* something about your suffering I do not any longer need to *feel* badly about it. But what is it that I want to do about it? What difference do I discern as that which I want (or ought) to make? It will not do to say that obviously I want to remove your suffering. If we can generalize helpfully at all here we should have to say something like this: Suffering is to be attacked where it obscures, intercepts or interdicts significant human action. For suffering as such is not the greatest enemy of the good. That is the paralysis of action, failure of energy and the depletion of natural resources which suffering *may* produce. Therefore it is not suffering that we ought so greatly dread but the loss of potency for the good which it may inflict on us. Suffering can indeed produce that loss. That is not a necessary consequence of any form of suffering, except despair.

Accordingly the greater the probability of the failure of potency for the good, the greater the demands placed upon sympathy and thereafter upon intercession—the prayer and the grace-proportioned deed. What is sought in intercession, above everything else, is deliverance of the other from alienation from the good. No creature can deliver another from that living death. The intercessor makes that deliverance his one increasing passion, until it is accomplished or his life is spent. "Father into thy hands . . ."

But surely when the kingdom of glory has taken up human history entire there will be no need for intercession. Our spirits have long been nourished by the glorious scriptural visions of that sublime state of affairs. No night there. No more crying, no desolating grief; because no death, no pain of separation or diminution.

All that is needed for an adequate reproof for this eschatological error (not the visions, the theology) is discoverable in the paradigmatic intercession, John 17. Here is portrayed the eschatological perfection of intercession. Christ the Lord no longer enters the lists against evil of unnameable monstrosity. He intercedes for the sanctification of the saints. They are not yet in the heaven to which the intercessor shortly returns— though not until he has been lifted high on the awful ransoming cross. They have been given supernatural powers to go with a supernatural vocation. So Christ does not intercede for their salvation. He intercedes in behalf of their kingdom work.

What does this mean, eschatologically? It means we need not represent the kingdom of glory as imperfectly free of the shadows of evil, to make place for intercession there. Let the light of heaven be ever so bright, so long as creaturely freedom obtains beneath it the possibility of the paralysis described above must also remain, the negative appropriation of suffering, allowing suffering to isolate or fragment the potency for the good. But, you say, how could there possibly be any suffering in the kingdom of glory?

That question indicates several things, beginning with a strange view of how in heaven *glory* is related to *solicitude:* when glory obtains, solicitude ends. Surely something is seriously amiss in such a view, and not least an obscure understanding of creativity and recreativity as God's eternal concerns. Recreativity (redemption) is best conceived as a transmutation of created elements, rather than as an upward-moving abolition of them *(aufheben),* there can be no end of God's solicitude for the integrity of his creatures, no matter how fierce the transmuting fires of his love.

The question also implies an unquestioned and unexamined confidence that the kingdom of glory allows no place for work. Excessively activistic souls in this world quite give their game away when they portray the world to come as a realm of eternal rest where the most that is demanded as an outlay of effort is an occasional hymn-sing around the throne of light. We have a right to question such expectations. Shall we then be past all caring for one another, in the strong sense of "care," that is looking out for the other, being solicitous for him, living for and toward the perfecting of his creative potentialities?

Surely our hope in Christ does not run toward the overcoming of sympathy. For this same Christ, on that night in which he was betrayed, in utmost grace prayed for the unity of all whom God has called. "I pray that they may be one even as we are one." There is a source of great and pious bafflement here. Why does Christ need to *pray* for that unity, when he *is* that unity? Is he blind to the power of his own being? Or is he there giving fullest expression to that power, the same being the perfectly indwelling grace of God? Surely in good faith we must answer *Yes* to that question. And it is the clue to the eschato-logical perfection of intercession. Interceding for the other, be he saint or unshriven sinner, is the essence of the calling in Christ, on earth as it is in heaven, now and always. This runs far beyond and above "doing what comes naturally." It is, rather, doing what comes gracefully.

A prior question has gone unattended. What, suffering in heaven? Yes, I think so: the suffering inescapably bound up in freeing creative good from crippling limitations. But how do *they* get into the kingdom of glory? On human feet. It is the kingdom of glory because the mediating good no longer must work in the dark to find and release potency for good. But that work still goes on. The joy of it is that it goes on within horizons behind which no hostile clouds lurk.

I have not intended to deal harshly with the eschatological assault on intercession. Who can seriously or honestly advertise his immunity to every false eschatology, in our time in this world? The multiplication and intensification of cultural crises places an immediate and great premium on every kind of inter-cessory action; but not only because the victims of social systems in conflict threaten to become more numerous than the sands of the earth's seas. There is the further reason that the ancient barriers against submergence in disaster—race, religion, class, power, wealth—are crumbling everywhere; and there is no safety for the happy few.

Our prayers do then, inevitably, take on an element of desperation: the needs are enormous, and tomorrow may be too late—for us!

It is not in itself a failure of charity that prompts one to say that desperation is poor stuff with which to mount inter-cessory prayer. And it is not in itself unreasonable to predict that the desperate urgency with which intercession is launched today will yield quite easily tomorrow to a longing to be done with it, either because we cannot see that it has done anything, or because we cannot endure any longer the terrors and temptations of a world in crisis, and thereupon retire into religious privacy to caress the golden images of Heaven all day every day.

John 17 breathes a joy not of this world. Yet wherever the mind of Christ bodily dwells that joy permeates the state of affairs. For that emotion is the blessed correlate of life poured out freely for the blessing of the world. That is the essence of intercession. That is the perfection of sympathy.

an age of change and its challenge to prayer

KATHARINE R. HANLEY

Unlike many of the other speakers at this Symposium, I do not stand before you in the role of professional theologian. Nor have I experienced the type of prolonged formal religious training in which many of you have engaged. I speak rather as a philosopher, a woman and a person who has long been deeply concerned with personal prayer in the course of my life. Personal experience and philosophic reflection, however, are not two different sources from which I shall draw my reflections. In my case, at least (as in that of many contemporary philosophers), they are one. If anything characterizes today's phenomenological philosophy in Europe, where I received six years of my training, it is a method of reflection, in which philosophic understanding is born from attention to concrete actions of life itself. My effort today, therefore, will simply be to reflect with you on the reality of Christian prayer, as each of us has known it, with the confidence that philosophy's point of view, or its specific stance before reality, can contribute new light on a form of human involvement without which each of our lives would be strangely empty, reduced by a full dimension.

Before turning our attention directly to the experience of personal prayer, I would like to make one comment on the context in which all efforts to realize values are cast today. Is it too much to say that every value, and also the value of our prayer, are caught up in a wave of change? The value of prayer itself, or better perhaps our understanding and appreciation of its value, is in a state of transition. I risk stating the truism not because contemporary philosophy or value theory is suddenly becoming aware of the imposing proportions of change, but more importantly because it is finally constructing a method for directing change into channels that will nourish man rather than impoverish him. That method consists in delving below the level of fluid actions and reactions among men who pray in the effort to discern what positive forces are at work, what new aspirations impel contemporary religious man. Success in discerning these forms and aspirations will result not in devaluating prayer, nor negating any of its values, but in recognizing those forms and features in which prayer can alone thrive and gain vitality in the urbanized air of twentieth-century America.

My procedure, therefore, will be quite straightforward. I propose, first of all, to consider what I suggest are the most important challenges that a man or woman must meet in the effort to pray in our age of transition. I will analyze those challenges from two points of view. First, I shall very briefly attempt to trace how today's questioning of prayer arises from man's new image of what must be avoided at all costs if he is to escape estrangement. Secondly, and this will form the greater bulk of my remarks, I will attempt to identify those positive features of man's self-image and aspirations which animate his questioning of past prayer and prefigure a form which will enrich and expand his deepest potentialities. In sum I shall attempt to draw a sketch of the nature of prayer—if not new in its broad outlines, new at least in the emphasis it gives to certain elements in the constellation of things prayer is. If my method is successful, this sketch will respond to legitimate aspirations to find full meaning in our cooperative efforts at union with God.

In my estimation then, challenges arise to the practice of prayer as we have known it, from three identifiable quarters. The first challenge, if not the most important one, is directed at specific forms and rituals of prayer. We have become uneasy with particular devotions, once so familiar. Novenas, recitations of the rosary, litanies, aspirations, communions of devotion have lost their enchantment for young adults. They have dropped from the pedagogy of modern catechetics.

More importantly, to my mind, the very regularity of prayerful practices, once a principle of spiritual direction, is subject to challenge. The repetitious regularity of morning offering, grace at meals, prayer before class, daily meditation, periodic days of recollection, annual closed retreat leave one ill at ease because of their seeming artificiality and formalism, their lack of spontaneity.

Lastly, and most importantly, because it tests the eyes of faith whereby we discern God's face, a twofold challenge confronts our practice of prayer from the alleged modern death of God. It may seem strange that I introduce an esoteric movement in technical theology as a challenge to the normal Christian's untechnical life of prayer, and yet I am convinced that currents in technical theology as well as in philosophy give voice to ideals and aspirations present in the cultural life of a whole people. The "death of God" movement takes shape as a challenge to the reality, vitality and meaningfulness of man's contact with one so transcendent that no human concept can glimpse him as he is. And it supplies a substitute target for the energies previously expended in intellectual contemplation. In its extreme, it would turn man from the hidden absent God exclusively to the task of binding up the wounds and reshaping the face of our broken human world.

Even so schematic an outline as this, points up the contemporary challenges to private prayer as formidable. I suspect that no one of us, indeed no Christian, is untouched by it. Some have reacted with decisiveness, if not with discernment, in abandoning the practice altogether, as a contentless, ritualistic talking to oneself. Others have scuttled fixed forms like the rosary or have decided in principle not to be regular with their practices. Some have maintained their habitual course with no more than the suspicion of fear and distrust of the validity of their practices.

This brings us to the central concern of our paper. What is prayer, what should prayer be in the effort to meet challenges which spring from the spirit of our times? As I mentioned above, what I would like to do in the remainder of these reflections is to delve below the level of the challenges mentioned, in order to understand and evaluate what modern man is trying to avoid in his questioning of prayer, and to discern the directions his new aspirations take as he attempts to pray anew.

What are the forces at work, what are the features of contemporary man's self-image, that force him to reevaluate the worth of standard rituals and fixed forms to express his sentiments toward God? Is modern man so unprincipled or haphazard in his conduct that any discipline of regular prayer is inevitably frustrating? For purposes of economy we can consider these first two challenges together, since both bear on the verbal structure and temporal sequence of our efforts at union with God.

If I read modern man correctly, he has learned a justified fear of the artificial, the strained, the contrived and the un-natural. He distrusts the formula simply because it is a formula, the gesture simply because it is a gesture. He knows that regimen inevitably tends to dominate him and diminish his total human powers rather than to channel and stimulate them. And these are legitimate fears.

In their place he esteems what is spontaneous, genuine, direct and natural. He wants his actions to be his, his faithfulness a renewed commitment of freedom. He abhors entanglement with the superficial, for he yearns to engage himself in what is essential. Thus he wants his actions, attitudes and involvements to flow from a genuine inner disposition, a personal engagement of freedom. And he wants his faithfulness to have the genuine character of spontaneity and wholeness which can arise only from a personal commitment. He wants the regularity in practice to flow from a living bond of commitment that resources and invites creative fidelity.

Is it possible for us to evolve forms of prayer in which we can succeed in avoiding the formalism and emptiness that modern man so justly fears, at the same time that we realize the spontaneity and personal engagement we have learned to value? The task is a formidable one because it confronts us with the paradoxical character of all language and gesture, with the ambiguous role which habit plays in the course of human growth. Words and gestures have the mysterious power of carry-ing meaning, and therefore run the perpetual risk of losing meaning by our mindless use of them. The fidelity and regularity which stems from stable character and commitment, ever threaten to rob a man of his ability to engage himself freely, out of the center of his own initiative. Yet for prayer to meet modern man's needs, it must escape the threat of formalism and magic; it must express a creative gift of self.

I suggest that there is no theoretic prescription which will automatically guarantee that this will take place. The most we can do is testify that it can take place—and pledge confidence in God's conspiring to make it so.

When one poses or recalls the act, I pray, one notices the following. Although prayer finds its expression in particular acts of subjectivity, such as speaking, imagining, willing, loving, questioning or understanding; the act, I pray, differs decisively from any other act of talking, doing, thinking or deciding for prayer begins with and keeps as its central dynamism an invocation of divine presence.

The beginning of prayer is a movement of relaxation or abandon to an englobing and inward presence. The mainstream of prayer as an act of human subjectivity is maintaining an availibility of openness and a quest of invocation, which actively invites the gratuitous favor of God's presence.

No casual nod, perfunctory statement or hollow gesture; prayer arises from and engages the core of one's personality and freedom. In entering into prayer, one pulls together his resources and gathers himself at the very center of his personhood to turn his attention and focus his whole subjectivity in a deeply personal act of invocation that expresses his total availability and appeal.

The distinctive threshold and heart of prayer is an active awaiting and grateful welcoming of divine reality as a presence with and for me. Pursuing this perspective we see prayer emerge as an interpersonal act. For the one who prays seeks divine reality as a presence, both as object of his invocation and as inward influx conspiring in his act of prayer. In praying one uses human activities in his or her attempt to grasp an aspect of divine reality, yet one finds these efforts graced with an enlightenment of faith, an ardor of love, or an intimacy of union that is other and more than the result of one efforts alone. Indeed, the Spirit prays in us. Thus one finds that prayer arises from within, yet draws on resources that are other than one's own. Prayer emerges as a coauthored work. For in prayer, God's presence is given not only as object of encounter but also as an influx of eminently personalizing forces which inspire, animate, sustain and actualize the most fundamental aspirations that one owns.

No isolated act, nor mere exercise of particular human faculties, prayer is rather the most whole act a human person can pose. It arises in and engages the deepest center of one's personhood. Relating thus to one's God, one speaks the language and accomplishes the reality of love. In reverent adoration and profound gratitude prayer accomplishes the radical and total gift of self. As an encounter with one's God, prayer follows the logic of love that leads to total self gift. To pray is to open oneself and one's life totally to God. The loving response to his gratuitous presence and invitation is total commitment to live one's life with and for God. To speak reciprocally the self gift of love is to constitute a bond which is a total permanent union.

Yet prayer for all its uniqueness and wholeness as an act of total self gift or a life of unlimited commitment to God, has the condition of all things human. It remains an irrevocable permanent disposition of one's life and person, yet it aspires and needs to grow and develop through renewed acts of creative fidelity that express love and keep its source a living presence.

Reflection discloses some deeper traits of the essence of prayer, which suggest new emphases in our understanding of its nature and practice. Not merely a series of repeated separate acts, nor these merely as incomplete gestures exercising only certain human faculties, nor merely man's sole efforts alone; the heart and abiding reality of prayer emerges rather as a co-authored whole and habitual orientation of one's life, a fundamental attitude that expresses and accomplishes a total gift of self, realized intersubjectively in a living bond of reciprocal commitment and interaction.

Prayer is a personal life orientation that would be constant, permanent and total union. Yet prayer, like all things human must grow, find new expression, be renewed and refreshed. The ardor for intimacy and union may inspire its renewals. The desire for more complete response leads to new expressions, and the aspiration for creative fidelity in new and changing circumstances invites the renewal of invocation for fuller and fresh inward presence of divine love and light. Thus the wellspring and vitality for prayer's regularity and expression is the ardor and inward dynamism of a life of love. Flowing thus, one's constancy and fidelity is more personal, freer and more spontaneous. Indeed the forms of expression will be more varied, apt and wisely chosen; and the rhythm may be less mathematical and closer to the supple timing of fidelity in interpersonal love throughout the changing circumstances and different phases of growth in life.

The third source of challenge to our prayer life today is more subtle in its influence than any frontal attack against specific practices against fidelity and constancy in our efforts. It is the challenge I mentioned above as connected with the death of God movement in technical philosophy and theology. The threat it poses to prayer is subtle because it is comprehensive. It calls for a rethinking of man's relation to the transcendent God as well as his relation to nature, societies and mundane history. At its deepest level it marks the crystalization of a conception of man that has been gestating for a century, an image that includes a newly harmonized view of man's nature and a shift in emphasis as to what constitutes his Christian task.

Modern man has given new emphasis to the centuries-old controversy over the role of prayer and action within Christian life. For the more Christians allowed God to *absent* himself from civilization, to become hidden beneath the spectacular accomplishments of men shaping history, the more man's suspicion grew that prayer was irrelevant to the urgent business of Christian living. The more man sensed his essential responsibility to employ his imagination, his physical strength, his intelligence and the warmth of his compassion to shape the lines of our human city, the more prayer seemed an ineffectual delusion, a purely intellectual exercise which left man's larger reserves of energy unspent.

Today's prayer must not give substance to our contemporary fears of irrelevance; it must do no violence to the wholeness of our nature as spirit-incarnate; it must, in practice if not in theory, accept a full alliance with worldly engagement. Our prayerful regard of God must not turn our eyes from worldly tasks, but sharpen our vision of what must be done. "Raising our hearts and minds to God" must remain a valid metaphor to the extent that we acknowledge, even heighten, our sense of God's transcendence. But it must be broadened to acknowledge that even the transcendent can be prayed to only as a transcendent-for-me, a Beyond whose presence has become experiential.

Once again, I have no foolproof formula according to which such prayer will be realized. I can only outline some features I have observed, which indicate that authentic prayer, far from countering modern man's aspirations, is rather their fulfillment.

Let us reflect again upon the contours of the experience: I pray. As noticed above, the act of prayer constitutes a manner of making oneself available and permeable to God, far different from the openness we acknowledge to any other reality of our experience. To call upon God at all is to call upon him as mysteriously other than any familiar friend or ally or accomplice. Even in its most intense realizations of union, prayer includes the unmistakeable awareness that God's Being wonderfully surpasses what we know or fathom of him. The overflow or surplus of God's transcendent Being over any other always gives genuine prayer an overtone of reverence, which is the echo of our faith in the unseen. Faith's reverence is spoken each time we say "My Lord and my God." To pray however, is not merely to open oneself reverently to the All-Holy, in its fullest form prayer issues a welcome which is definitive, unreserved, without temporal limit. None but the transcendent justifies an unreserved invocation for a totally unqualified welcome to our human heart.

Every individual act of prayer, therefore, affirms a permanent disposition, a fundamental orientation of self which ideally pledges all one's reserves and for all time.

Yet, paradoxically, a prayer which renders one completely available to the presence of the transcendent, increases rather than diminishes one's energy for human concerns. For the God we search and invoke has shown himself to be faithfully and intimately present with and for man. Our Christian God is no mere competitor to worldly causes in vying for our loyalty; he showed himself in Christ, the Sacrament of our encounter, as authoring all causes and attracting all movements which tend to renew the earth.

Because the God we meet in prayer does not exist on the same level as the world, he is no competitor to the world. Nor is our human activity of prayer engaged in any competition with other human interests or projects. Prayer is rather an act of mediation between God and man's world. The one who prays reaches out to embrace God and all humanity. He strives to effect an interaction between the bounty, providence and mercy of God and the needs, sufferings and aspirations of all men. Thus in both one's being and activity the one who prays is intermediary. The one who prays is in his or her own being both the loneliness and the home, the drowning shipwreck and the haven, the poverty and the shareholder of bounty. And in the activity of prayer one is united with the needs, projects and hopes of fellowmen, yet moreover united to Christ in God inviting and channeling the divine compassion to intervene—sustaining men's hopes, conspiring toward their accomplishment and humanizing people so that their spirit of compassion and bond of unity increases.

This trait of mediation is always essential to prayer. The forms of its realization will vary. Emphasis on one direction or another in the lives of different individuals will depend on temperament, circumstances and individual choice of a life style. Prayer is incipient love, and love is never exclusive or isolationist. It embraces all. It acts toward all.

When prayer begins as we have described it, there is a sense in which action itself becomes prayer. Not that action is an arbitrary substitute for prayer—but it is an integrating element in that fundamental disposition of availability to God and invocation of him, with all his salvific designs on man, that makes any prayer a prayer. The exercise of any noble human function can body forth one's prayerful availability to God and mankind. Defending indigents' cases in court, firming up the economy of a nation, providing light to darkened minds or productive skills to awkward hands—all of these can be expressions, incarnate gestures, expressing and nourishing one's fundamental availability to a God concerned with human well-being.

The give and take of daily encounters with people, the up and down, success and failure in work projects may be the crucible of action in which one's dedication is purified, one's personality transformed from a selfish solipsism to generous service and understanding reverent love.

But if action in the sense described can be prayer, it is equally true that only in the setting of prayer can human action realize its full beauty and worth. If our efforts to heal the ills of mankind are not nourished by a deeper commitment, if our ultimate hopes and efforts to promote fullness of life do not depend on the gift of divine reality as participable by man, then indeed their worth is fragile; ultimate hope is no more than a wager against ultimate despair over the entire human enterprise.

Yet in prayer, one develops a new vision and valuation of the worldly and human. The goodness and possibilities of worldly and human activities are seen in convergence with a way of loving and a dignity—even an eminent fullness of life that Christ has shown and continues to offer for our participation and extension in the Spirit.

I pray. That is, I actively prepare myself to welcome, with all my gifts and shortcomings, the presence of the All-Holy. I invoke his presence, and with his conspiring, mediate his salvific designs to a world in the making. Such a prayer does not exercise my mind alone, nor does it occur at discreet moments of recollection or studied attention. It is capable of engaging all the resources of mind and heart and body of each individual who prays. It is integral in its self donation; integral in the transformation it can work in the whole person; integral in the response and vision it animates.

For, while ever remaining reverent of the divine transcendence, a life of prayer cultivates and increases our sensitivity to the presence of divine reality by way of immanence. One sees God in his active concern with and for man toward realizing the fullness of life open to him. One sees worldly and human activities as promotions and realizations of this wholeness of being. Thus one's involvement in life grasps and responds to all that is there. One's human and worldly actions become responses of love for man in God, and one's vision and estimation of human and worldly values gratefully reverence the gifts of God and their author.

Let us gather the main lines sketching features of prayer as envisaged according to modern man's aspirations. Prayer emerges as a jointly sourced, total gift of self, that has the constancy and union of love; a total permanent commitment, whose ardor and inner dynamism seeks growth and resources fresh expressions and creative incarnations; an intersubjective reality whereby God is inwardly present both as object and source of vision, love and action; a whole elevation whereby one is totally open to God and fully available to integrally love and serve man; a gift of God that man actively invokes and gratuitously receives, one that transforms his being, vision and action while calling for man's co-creation of its expressions and incarnations.

We live in an age of transition. Christian prayer itself is no exception to the law of evolution. Its practices are being reevaluated, its regular place in the rhythm of life has been disturbed. Its relevance has been challenged in a world whose secular needs must be met by secular competence.

Yet beneath these challenges, I am convinced, there is at work a salutary distrust of emphases in prayer which should be disturbed. More importantly, there are aspirations emerging for an understanding and practice of prayer which will constitute a genuine renewal, that is, a reemphasis on elements within the experience of prayer which previous culture, being different, could not have emphasized.

Ours is an age of personalism (some say of romanticism). It values frankness without formalism or formality. Sad experience has taught us to fear the lock-step of the past and the programmed of the future. Willy-nilly we are compelled to the gigantic task of tending society's long standing and newly developing ills. At our best we know the meaning of self-giving, and we are constant and loyal to commitments met.

"Prayer" has no predetermined meaning, fulfilled each time you or I invoke God's holy name. Prayers can be empty formulas or mental gymnastics or flight from pressing responsibility toward our brothers. But it also can be the deepest of inter-personal encounters which will at times seek expression in inadequate words, at times nourish productivity for our fellow man as no humanistic motive can. It can be rich enough to stimulate our sense of fidelity to the point where abandoning or neglecting it becomes unthinkable.

As in other ages, so in ours, the words "I pray" can be the fulfillment of man's finest aspirations. It is our decision and the conspiring of God, which can make them so.

BIOGRAPHICAL NOTES

CHRISTOPHER F. MOONEY, S.J.: President of Woodstock College, he pursued his doctoral studies in Paris at the Institut Catholique. He later joined Fordham University's Department of Theology, becoming its Chairman in 1965. His publications have appeared in *Thought, Downside Review, Continuum, Christianity and Crisis* and elsewhere, and he is the author of *Teilhard de Chardin and the Mystery of Christ*. As Director of the Cardinal Bea Institute, he has edited a volume of Institute lectures entitled *The Presence and Absence of God*.

THOMAS E. CLARKE, S.J.: Professor of Systematic Theology at Woodstock College, he received his S.T.D. from the Gregorian University in Rome. Associate Editor of *America*, he has also written for *Theological Studies, Commonweal, Thought* and other journals, and is co-author, with James M. Carmody, S.J., of *Christ and His Mission* and *Word and Redeemer*. He is currently preparing a monograph for the *Catholic Theological Encyclopedia* on "Jesus Christ in Dogmatic Theology." In the spring of 1968, Father Clarke was Visiting Professor of Theology at Fordham University.

JEAN LECLERQ, O.S.B.: One of the world's leading authorities on monasticism, especially its culture and spirituality, he entered the Benedictine Abbey of Clervaux in 1928, and later studied in Rome and Paris under such masters as Arquilliere, Gilson, Halphen and Samaran. His publications number in the hundreds, but he is best known to the English reading public for *The Love of Learning and the Desire for God*, a classic study of medieval monasticism. Some of his other books are *The Life of Perfection, Liturgical and Biblical Prayer*, and *History and Mystery: Essays on Monastic Culture*.

DAVID M. STANLEY, S.J.: Having obtained his S.T.L. from St. Louis University and his S.S.D. from the Pontifical Biblical

Institute in Rome, he is currently Professor of New Testament Studies at Regis College in Ontario, Canada. He was, for several years, Associate Professor of New Testament Studies at the State University of Iowa. In addition to numerous articles in *America, Worship, Concilium, Scripture* and other journals, Father Stanley has written several books: *Christ's Resurrection in Pauline Soteriology, The Apostolic Church in the New Testament,* and *A Modern Scriptural Approach to the Spiritual Exercises.*

ROBERT J. O'CONNELL, S.J.: The recipient of a Ph.D. from the Sorbonne, he is Associate Professor of Philosophy at Fordham University, specializing in the Philosophy of Man. He has written extensively for *International Philosophical Quarterly, Thought* and other journals, and has lectured widely on St. Augustine and Teilhard de Chardin. His *St. Augustine's Confessions* and *St. Augustine's Early Theory of Man* were both recently published by the Harvard University Press.

JULIAN N. HARTT: An ordained minister in the Methodist Church, he is a specialist in Christian dogmatics and philosophical theology, lecturing more recently on the religious aspects of contemporary culture. Professor Hartt joined the faculty of Berea College in 1940 after receiving his doctorate from Yale. He is presently Noah Porter Professor of Philosophical Theology at the Yale Divinity School and Chairman of the University's Department of Religious Studies. A member of numerous societies and associations, he has authored, among other works, *The Lost Image of Man, Being Known and Being Revealed,* and *A Christian Criticism of American Culture.*

KATHARINE R. HANLEY: Associate Professor of Philosophy at Le Moyne College in Syracuse, New York, she also serves as Chairman of the Department of Philosophy. A graduate of Manhattanville College, Miss Hanley received her Ph.D. from Louvain University in 1961. She has written articles on "Existentialism" and "Gabriel Marcel: Man Before the Alleged Death of God," and more recently authored, together with J. Donald Monan, S.J., *A Prelude to Metaphysics.*